Sedatives
and Hypnotics
Deadly Downers

ILLICIT AND MISUSED DRUGS

ILLICIT AND MISUSED DRUGS
Sedatives
and Hypnotics
Deadly Downers

by Ida Walker

Mason Crest

Mason Crest
370 Reed Road
Broomall, Pennsylvania 19008
www.masoncrest.com

Printed in the Hashemite Kingdom of Jordan.

First printing
9 8 7 6 5 4 3 2 1

Library of Congress Cataloging-in-Publication Data

Walker, Ida.
Sedatives and hypnotics : deadly downers / by Ida Walker.
    p. cm. — (Illicit and misused drugs)
Includes bibliographical references and index.
ISBN 978-1-4222-2440-3 (hardcover)
ISBN 978-1-4222-2424-3 (hardcover series)
ISBN 978-1-4222-9304-1 (ebook)
1. Sedatives—Juvenile literature. 2. Hypnotics—Juvenile litera-
ture. I. Title.
 RM325.W35 2012
 615.7'82—dc23
                                       2011042530

Interior design by Benjamin Stewart.
Cover design by Torque Advertising + Design.
Produced by Harding House Publishing Services, Inc.
www.hardinghousepages.com

This book is meant to educate and should not be used as an alternative to appropriate medical care. Its creators have made every effort to ensure that the
information presented is accurate—but it is not intended to substitute for the
help and services of trained professionals.

CONTENTS

INTRODUCTION

Addicting drugs are among the greatest challenges to health, well-being, and the sense of independence and freedom for which we all strive—and yet these drugs are present in the everyday lives of most people. Almost every home has alcohol or tobacco waiting to be used, and has medicine cabinets stocked with possibly outdated but still potentially deadly drugs. Almost everyone has a friend or loved one with an addiction-related problem. Almost everyone seems to have a solution neatly summarized by word or phrase: medicalization, legalization, criminalization, war-on-drugs.

For better and for worse, drug information seems to be everywhere, but what information sources can you trust? How do you separate misinformation (whether deliberate or born of ignorance and prejudice) from the facts? Are prescription drugs safer than "street" drugs? Is occasional drug use really harmful? Is cigarette smoking more addictive than heroin? Is marijuana safer than alcohol? Are the harms caused by drug use limited to the users? Can some people become addicted following just a few exposures? Is treatment or counseling just for those with serious addiction problems?

These are just a few of the many questions addressed in this series. It is an empowering series because it provides the information and perspectives that can help people come to their own opinions and find answers to the challenges posed by drugs in their own lives. The series also provides further resources for information and assistance, recognizing that no single source has all the answers. It should be of interest and relevance to areas of study spanning biology, chemistry, history, health, social studies and more. Its efforts to provide a real-world context for the information that is clearly presented but not overly simplified should be appreciated by students, teachers, and parents.

The series is especially commendable in that it does not pretend to pose easy answers or imply that all decisions can be made on the basis of simple facts: some challenges have no immediate or simple solutions, and some solutions will need to rely as much upon basic values as basic facts. Despite this, the series should help to at least provide a foundation of knowledge. In the end, it may help as much by pointing out where the solutions are not simple, obvious, or known to work. In fact, at many points, the reader is challenged to think for him- or herself by being asked what his or her opinion is.

A core concept of the series is to recognize that we will never have all the facts, and many of the decisions will never be easy. Hopefully, however, armed with information, perspective, and resources, readers will be better prepared for taking on the challenges posed by addictive drugs in everyday life.

— *Jack E. Henningfield, Ph.D.*

1 Sedatives and Hypnotics: What They Are

Ahh. The day is over, and you're ready for a long night's sleep. You climb into bed, punch the pillow a few times to get it "just right," and settle in. The temperature in the room is just the way you like it, and the room is dark. You've done everything the doctor suggested for getting a good night's sleep, so you settle in, waiting for sleep to overtake you.

But as soon as your head hits the pillow, your mind starts racing. The worries of the day—real and imagined—leap to the forefront of your consciousness. *How am I ever going to get to sleep? I have to be at my peak tomorrow for the test; I really need to sleep.* You stumble out of bed and make your way to the medicine cabinet in the bathroom.

This is your first college party, and to say you are looking forward to it would be a major understatement. You have

Benzodiazepine is a sedative that when used as a "date-rape drug," denies a young woman her right to say, "No!"

a new outfit, sure, but the biggest thing is that Evan Ford has asked you to go with him. The Evan Ford, one of the most popular guys in school!

Oh, it is so hot in here, you think after a few dances on the crowded floor. Evan must have read your mind: "Let's take a break. I'll get us something to drink." You follow him off the dance floor to a group of your friends. He and his buddies go off to get cold beers, which you drink enthusiastically.

I-I-I don't feel right. Don't let me get sick tonight of all nights. "Evan . . ."

The people in both of these fictional stories represent two types of potential users of sedative-hypnotic medication. In the first story, the young man may find relief by taking a prescription sleeping or anti-anxiety medication. He's tried his doctor's other suggestions, but they don't seem to be working. He may find that a prescription for a benzodiazepine will help him sleep.

Sadly, the teenage girl at the dance wasn't given the chance to make a decision about taking a drug. "Mr. Popular" slipped a benzodiazepine called Rohypnol® into her beer. And, they don't call it the "date-rape drug" without a reason.

Along with barbiturates, benzodiazepine belongs to a medication classification called sedative-hypnotics. They act as depressants on the central nervous system (CNS), slowing down some of its actions. The primary purpose of these depressants is in the treatment of **anxiety** and sleep disorders. Some very popular medications (just count the number of commercials for prescription sleeping medications you see on television if you have any doubts) are sedative-hypnotics that have a long **pharmacological** history.

Sedative-Hypnotics

barbiturates: phenobarbital, amobarbital, secobarbital
benzodiazepines: Valium®, Ativan®, Librium®, Xanax®
chloral hydrate: Somnos®
others: glutethimide (Doriden®); methaqualone (Quaaludes®); meprobamate (Miltown®); ethchlorvynol (Placidyl®); flunitrazepam (Rohypnol®); gamma-hydroxybutyrate (GHB, Liquid X, Easy Lay)

The Beginning

Stress, anxiety, and sleep disorders cross cultural barriers and times. Each era has had its stressors—survival, war, poverty, high-tech—and individuals have sought methods of dealing with that stress and its fallout. One of the earliest "cures" for insomnia, anxiety, and stress was alcohol. No one knows for certain when alcohol was first used as a beverage, but Stone Age beer jugs discovered on archaeological expeditions show that civilizations fermented beverages during the Neolithic period (around 10,000 BCE).

Others used techniques many today would call "alternative" methods. Meditation, prayer, yoga, and exercise were just some of the ways people have dealt with—and continue to deal with—stress, anxiety, and insomnia.

Sometimes, those methods don't work, or as in the case of alcohol, they come with a host of problems themselves. For many years, scientists searched for chemical methods to lessen stress, anxiety, and insomnia. These medications had different names throughout their development—downers, sedatives, hypnotics, anxiolytics, minor tranquilizers.

The oldest hypnotic, chloral hydrate, was *synthesized* in 1832. Remember in old black-and-white movies seeing

Seventeenth-century settlers in Jamestown brewed beer to help them deal with the stresses of early colonial life.

Dating Systems and Their Meaning

You might be accustomed to seeing dates expressed with the abbreviations BC or AD, as in the year 1000 BC or the year AD 1900. For centuries, this dating system has been the most common in the Western world. However, since BC and AD are based on Christianity (BC stands for Before Christ and AD stands for anno Domini, Latin for "in the year of our Lord"), many people now prefer to use abbreviations that people from all religions can be comfortable using. The abbreviations BCE (meaning Before Common Era) and CE (meaning Common Era) mark time in the same way (for example, 1000 BC is the same year as 1000 BCE, and AD 1900 is the same year as 1900 CE), but BCE and CE do not have the same religious overtones as BC and AD.

someone "slip a Mickey" into an alcoholic drink of an unsuspecting individual, who then passed out, often sliding to the floor for added dramatic effect? That was a Mickey Finn—chloral hydrate when mixed with alcohol. It is still available as a liquid or in gelatin pills. Known by the street names "knockout drops," or "Mickey Finn" when added to alcohol, it is in use today. Sodium bromide and potassium bromide were used as hypnotics and sedatives in the nineteenth and early twentieth centuries. Today, their use in humans is not as prevalent. Potassium bromide, however, is used in veterinary medicine. Evolution of sedatives and hypnotics has continued, and although medications such as gluthethimide, methaqualone, and meprobamate have shown effectiveness, two primary groups of depressants were developed, barbiturates and benzodiazipines.

Barbiturates

In 1864, the German chemist Johann Friedrich Wilhelm Adolf von Baeyer synthesized malonylurea caused by a reaction of urea, a nitrogen compound found in the urine of mammals and produced through protein decomposition, and malonic acid found in apples. No one knows exactly what the chemist was looking for, but his discovery

Who Was Mickey Finn?

Though "Mickey Finn" played an important role in many films of the thirties and forties, where did the name for a drug-laced alcoholic beverage originate? Well, no one knows for certain. One of the more popular theories is that it comes from an infamous Chicago bar, closed in 1903. Allegedly, the bar's customers were served drinks spiked with drugs, which caused them to become incapacitated. After the customers passed out, bar employees robbed them.

Brand Name vs. Generic Name

Talking about medications can be confusing because every drug has at least two names: its "generic name" and the "brand name" that the pharmaceutical company uses to market the drug. Generic names are based on the drug's chemical structure, while drug companies use brand names in order to inspire public recognition and loyalty for their products.

Adolf von Baeyer was a German chemist who created barbituric acid, creating the foundation for sedatives to be developed by later chemists.

was named barbituric acid because it was accomplished, according to legend anyway, on the Day of St. Barbara. Barbituric acid proved to have no medicinal value, but it led the way for other scientists to discover medically beneficial drugs.

In 1902, another German scientist, Hermann Emil Fischer, and German physiologist Joseph Freiherr von Mering discovered the medicinal properties of diethylbarbituric acid, which Fischer had previously discovered through synthesis. The new drug was found to be a hypnotic, bringing relaxation and drowsiness to those who took it. The following year, the pharmaceutical companies Merck and Bayer marketed Fischer and von Mering's discovery as a sleep-inducing medication under the brand name Veronal. It proved to be a big seller for the drug companies.

Despite its popularity and success as a hypnotic, Veronal was not without problems. The sleep-inducing effects came slowly, and they were even slower to wear off, sometimes causing users to sleep for up to thirty-six hours!

Work continued on the development of hypnotics, especially those based on diethlybarbituric acid. Three years after the discovery of diethylbarbituric acid, Fischer found that by replacing ethyl groups with propyl groups, the strength of the drug could be doubled. The new drug was marketed under the name Proponal.

Hermann Emil Fischer played a major role in developing the first sleep-inducing medication.

The search for new compounds was not limited to Fischer and those working with him. Two teams working independently—including the one headed by Fischer—continued working with forms of barbituric acid and created another new compound in 1912. The newly developed compound came from the synthesis of **chiral** phenylethylbarbituric acid. Called phenobarbital, the compound was marketed under the name Luminal. The benefits of this new drug were not limited to its value as a hypnotic. The compound also acted as an **anticonvulsant** when taken twice daily. At first the hypnotic effects of phenobarbital were a problem when the drug was prescribed primarily for its anticonvulsive properties. Further research found that by taking an **antihistamine** with phenobarbital, the sleep-inducing effects could be lessened without compromising the drug's **efficacy** as an anticonvulsant.

> **Fast Fact**
>
> High doses of barbiturates are used to accomplish physician-assisted suicides. Combined with a muscle relaxant, barbiturates are used in euthanasia and as part of the lethal injection cocktail used in capital punishment.

Researchers continued to improve and find new barbiturates. Some researchers went back to the beginning and found that the reasons why barbituric acid had no medicinal value and the sleep-inducing effects of Veronal took so long to occur were both caused by the drug's difficulty in getting from the gastrointestinal tract into the circulatory system.

In order for one substance to dissolve within another, they must share some similarity. Fatty molecules make up the vessels that act as passageways to the circulatory

Human beings have always struggled with insomnia and have turned to chemicals as a solution. Sleep-inducing medications are still being developed. One drawback that many have is that they make people too sleepy. Veronal, for instance, the earliest sleep-inducer, made people sleep for up to 36 hours!

system for the drugs. Barbituric acid is not fat *soluble*, and Veronal is only slightly soluble in fat. This means that crossing from the gastrointestinal tract and into the circulatory system was impossible for barbituric acid and took a long time for Veronal. To explain this concept using items with which you might be more familiar, take a fine mesh strainer and pour in a mixture of sand and cold water. Because sand (which represents barbituric acid in this example) will not dissolve, it will not pass through the holes of the strainer. Now, in a clean strainer, pour in a mixture of table sugar (representing Veronal) and cold water. The sugar will not pass through the holes

The barrier between the gastrointestinal system and the bloodstream acts like a strainer, making it more difficult or impossible for certain substance to pass into the circulatory system.

20 Chapter 1—Sedatives and Hypnotics: What They Are

Drug Approval

Before a drug can be marketed in the United States, the Food and Drug Administration (FDA) must officially approve it. Today's FDA is the primary consumer protection agency in the United States. Operating under the authority given it by the government, and guided by laws established throughout the twentieth century, the FDA has established a rigorous drug approval process that verifies the safety, effectiveness, and accuracy of labeling for any drug marketed in the United States.

While the United States has the FDA for the approval and regulation of drugs and medical devices, Canada has a similar organization called the Therapeutic Product Directorate (TPD). The TPD is a division of Health Canada, the Canadian government's department of health. The TPD regulates drugs, medical devices, disinfectants, and sanitizers with disinfectant claims. Some of the things that the TPD monitors are quality, effectiveness, and safety. Just as the FDA must approve new drugs in the United States, the TPD must approve new drugs in Canada before those drugs can enter the market.

immediately, but in time, it will dissolve and easily slip through the holes, just as Veronal eventually makes it into the body's bloodstream.

Once scientists knew why these drugs were not efficient, they had an idea as to what direction their efforts should take. They developed molecules that resembled the fatty ones making up the vessels. This change allowed drugs to enter the bloodstream quickly. Some of the drugs that have resulted are amobarbital (Amytal®), pentobarbital (Nembutal®), and secobarbital (Seconal®). Unfortunately, the effectiveness of these medications has also made them popular drugs for abuse. Shorter-acting barbiturates were also developed after the transmission solution was found. These include hexobarbital (Evipal®), thiopental (Pentothal®), and methohexital (Brevital®).

Barbiturates were providing relief to many who had been unable to get a restorative sleep. They also aided in the treatment of *seizure* disorders such as epilepsy. However, they were not without problems; they were addictive, and some individuals who were prescribed the medication could become addicted. The pills were also the tools of some who committed suicide, including the femme fatale actress of her time, Marilyn Monroe.

Table 1. Common Types of Barbiturates				
Barbiturate	**Synonyms**	**Drug Class**	**Brand Names**	**Street Names**
Allobarbital		CNS depressant; sedative-hypnotic		
Alphenal	Phenallymal	CNS depressant; sedative-hypnotic		
Amobarbital		Anticonvulsant; CNS depressant; sedative-hypnotic	Amytal, Tuinal (secobarbital with amobarbital)	Blue Heavens, Christmas Trees (Tuinal), Rainbows (Tuinal), Tooies (Tuinal)
Aprobarbital		CNS depressant; sedative-hypnotic	Alurate	
Barbital		CNS depressant; sedative-hypnotic	Veronal	
Butabarbital	Allybarbital	CNS depressant; sedative-hypnotic	Barbased, Busodium, Butalan, Butisol, Sarisol No. 2	Bute, Stoppers
Butethal	Butobarbital	CNS depressant; sedative-hypnotic		
Pentobarbital		Anticonvulsant; CNS depressant; sedative-hypnotic	Ancalixir, Nembutal, Nova Rectal, Novopentobarb	Nembies, Yellow Jackets
Phenobarbital		Anticonvulsant; antihyperbilirubinemic CNS depressant; sedative-hypnotic	Barbita, Luminal, Solfoton	Phennies
Secobarbital		Anticonvulsant; CNS depressant; sedative-hypnotic	Seconal, Novosecobarb, Tuinal (secobarbital with amobarbital)	Christmas Trees (Tuinal), Rainbows (Tuinal), Red Birds, Seggies, Red Devils, Reds, Tooies (Tuinal)
Source: Adpated from www.drugtestsuccess.com/barbiturates.htm				

Addiction vs. Dependence

Sometimes these words are used interchangeably. However, addiction is a primary, chronic, neurobiological disease, with genetic, psychosocial, and environmental factors influencing its development and manifestations. It is characterized by behaviors that include one or more of the following:

• impaired control over drug use
• compulsive use
• continued use despite harm
• craving

The American Psychiatric Association (APA) and World Health Organization (WHO) refer in their technical and diagnostic documents to this condition as "dependence." However, other medical professionals define physical dependence as a state of adaptation manifested by a drug class-specific withdrawal syndrome that can be produced by abrupt cessation, rapid dose reduction, decreasing blood level of drug and/or administration of an antagonist and is relieved by the readministration of the drug or another drug of the same pharmacologic class.

Today, barbiturates as a class are not as widely prescribed except for surgical procedures and as anticonvulsants. The discovery of barbiturates and the research conducted to improve their delivery and later to find a safer alternative to the drug, helped lead to the development of the primary class of sedative-hypnotics in use today—benzodiazepines.

Benzodiazepines

The discovery of benzodiazepines actually began as part of a doctoral research program in Krakow, Poland, in the late 1920s and early 1930s. As part of his research, scientist Leo Sternbach worked on benzheptoxdiazines, a group of chemical compounds. That study was set aside for twenty years, until Dr. Sternbach, now with the prestigious pharmaceutical company Hoffman LaRoche, began work on a drug that would replace barbiturates, whose dangers were well known by the medical and pharmaceutical companies by that time. He experimented by synthesizing different chemical compounds, but all proved to have no medicinal properties. In fact, some had no active properties at all. In 1954, when he added methylamine to one of his new compounds, the result was a white powder that dissolved in water. But before he could study his discovery further, other duties at Hoffman LaRoche required his attention, so it was set aside.

The methylamine-treated compound stayed on the sidelines until 1957, when a research assistant cleaned Dr. Sternbach's lab and brought it back to the doctor's attention. Dr. Sternbach conducted further research on his compound, called Ro-5-0690, and found that it had *calmative* properties, reducing stress and anxiety, and most important, without the potential side effects of the barbiturates. In 1960, the U.S. Food and Drug Administration (FDA) approved the new drug chlordiazepoxide—now marketed by Hoffman LaRoche as Librium®—for use as a tranquilizer and anti-anxiety medication.

After Librium hit the pharmaceutical market, other benzodiazepines quickly followed. In 1963, diazepam (Valium®) received FDA approval as primarily a treatment for anxiety. Nitrazepam (Mogadon®) was approved in 1965 and flurazepam (Dalmane®) received approval in 1973, both for the treatment of sleep-related illnesses.

Once health-care professionals had new alternatives to treat anxiety-, stress-, and sleep-related disorders, the number of prescriptions written for barbiturates was cut in half. After all, doctors believed that these new medi-

Leo Sternbach developed the tranquilizer named Librium.

When counting sheep doesn't work, benzodiazepines are the most commonly prescribed medications for individuals suffering from chronic insomnia.

cations were nonaddictive. While that still seems to be true, these drugs can create dependence. However, they are not as toxic as the barbiturates, and have proven to be an ineffective way to commit suicide.

Table 2. Common Benzodiazepines	
Generic Name	**Brand Name**
Lorazepam	Ativan
Prazepam	Centrax
Flurazepam	Dalmane
Quazepam	Dormalin
Triazolam	Halcion
Clonazepam	Klonopin, Rivotril
Bromazepam	Lexotan
Chlordiaepoxide	Librium
Nitrazepam	Mogadon
Halazepam	Paxipam
Estazolam	ProSom
Temazepam	Restoril
Flunitrazepam	Rohypnol*
Oxazepam	Serax, Serenid
Chlorazepate	Tranxene
Diazepam	Valium
Midazolam	Versed, Hypnovel
Alprazolam	Xanax
* Rohypnol has been outlawed in the United States and Canada, among other countries.	

Though there are now other options available for the treatment of these disorders, benzodiazepines are the most-often prescribed medications for these disorders. However, they might not be the best choice for all individuals and all symptoms. To be an active participant in the medical decision-making process, individuals must know how these medications work on the body, and the potential side effects that may result.

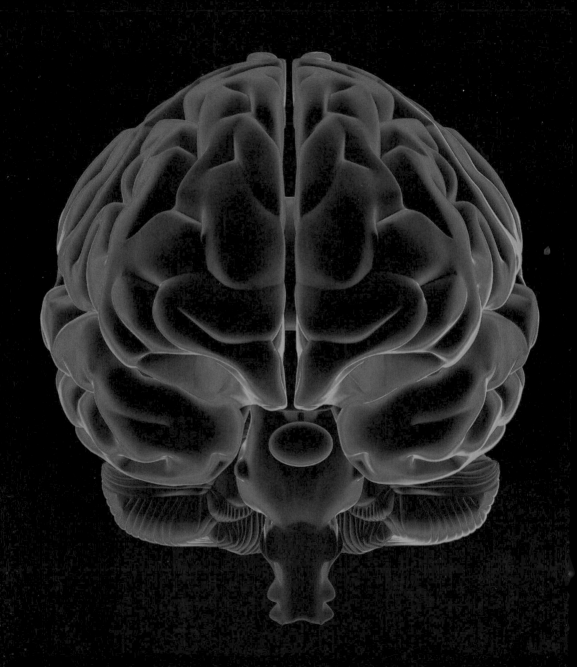

2 How They Work: The Good and the Bad

Sedative-hypnotics include all prescription sleeping medications and almost all prescription anti-anxiety drugs. Sedatives are used to treat agitation, reduce daytime activity, and reduce excitement, all with little impact on an individual's motor skills or mental functioning. Hypnotics cause drowsiness and help maintain a sleep state. Both sedatives and hypnotics are depressants that work on the body's central nervous system (CNS), slowing normal brain activity. Like most other depressants and other pharmaceuticals, they work on the neurotransmitter gamma-aminobutyric acid (GABA).

Neurotransmitters are chemicals that play an integral role in the brain's complex communication system. The basic unit of this messenger system is the neuron, or nerve cell. Messages are carried to the brain by presynaptic—sending—neurons. An electrical impulse is sent down the neuron's long, whip-like tail (axon) to the terminal buttons at the end. The neurons do not touch each other, so when the impulse reaches the dendrites (root-looking projections), it hitches a ride with the neurotransmitters across the synapse, the gap between the neurons, until it reaches its destination, the dendrites of the receiving—postsynaptic—neuron. With successful delivery, communication takes place, and an action is performed or a feeling is experienced.

GABA is an inhibitory neurotransmitter; it slows action. Both barbiturates and benzodiazepines increase GABA's ability to activate a special receptor called the GABA-A. Drugs in the sedative-hypnotic class change the receptor's makeup to make the binding process with GABA easier. Activating GABA-A causes an ion channel to open. This allows negatively charged chloride ions to enter the cell, thus slowing the activity in the neuron.

In general, these drugs:

- impair the sending and receiving of neurological impulses
- decrease the time before sleep comes
- increase the total amount of time spent sleeping

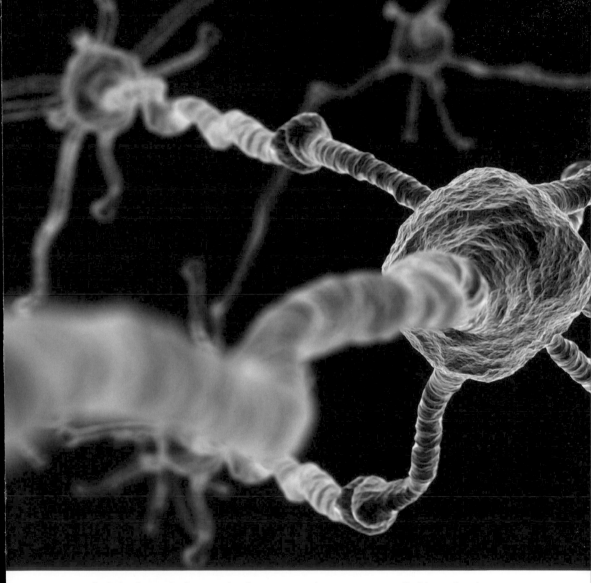

Sedative-hypnotic drugs make the messages between nerve cells (shown here) travel more slowly.

- diminish **REM** *sleep*
- lower blood pressure
- slow heart rate

Sedative-hypnotic drugs are used in the treatment of:

- *neuroses*
- anxiety
- depression
- *hypertension*
- *epilepsy*
- insomnia
- muscle tension

The two major classes of sedative-hypnotic drugs are barbiturates and benzodiazepines.

How They Work

Barbiturates

No matter what Abe did, he could not fall asleep. His insomnia had been going on for two years now, ever since his wife left him. He had tried natural remedies; he had taken over-the-counter medications like Sominex®; he had practiced various relaxation techniques—but nothing worked. Every five days or so, he would fall into a heavy slumber, as though he were drugged, and manage to sleep through the night. But the next night (and the night after that, and the one after that), his insomnia would be back. During the day, he was constantly exhausted. He was depressed and easily irritated, and he

Everyone has trouble sleeping from time to time, but chronic insomnia is a more serious condition that can get in the way of a person's ability to carry out ordinary, day-to-day tasks.

Sedatives and Hypnotics—Deadly Downers 33

When a person can't sleep at night, he may find himself drifting into sleep during the day, in the midst of other activities.

Barbiturates and World War II

One type of barbiturate, sodium pentothal, is sometimes referred to as truth serum. But, the truth is: the drug does not make people tell the truth. Someone under the influence of sodium pentothal may be less inhibited, however, and therefore more talkative.

The ability of barbiturates to allow access to an individual's subconscious was used to treat traumatized soldiers in World War II. Before barbiturates, these psychological areas were only accessible through dreams and "trances." Now, soldiers whose battle experiences were adversely affecting their lives, but who could not recall those horrors, could safely relive the experiences through barbiturates such as sodium pentothal and be treated by trained professionals.

knew his job was suffering as a result of his tiredness. His life seemed to have gone on a downward spiral, where everything just kept getting worse and worse.

Abe was desperate. He went to a doctor and tried various prescription sleep medications. Each time, he would think he had finally found the answer, only to have his insomnia return again in full force. Oh, the drugs helped Abe fall asleep—but after only a few hours of unconsciousness, he would be wide awake again, and he would stay that way for the rest of the night.

At last, his doctor prescribed a drug called Seconal. His doctor explained that the drug's real name was secobarbital, and that it was a form of barbiturate. When Abe took the medication at bedtime, it would help him fall asleep—and best of all, it would help him stay asleep through night. There was just one catch: Abe could only take the drug for a couple of weeks. If he took it longer, he would probably develop tolerance for the drug; in other words, he would have to take increasing amounts in order

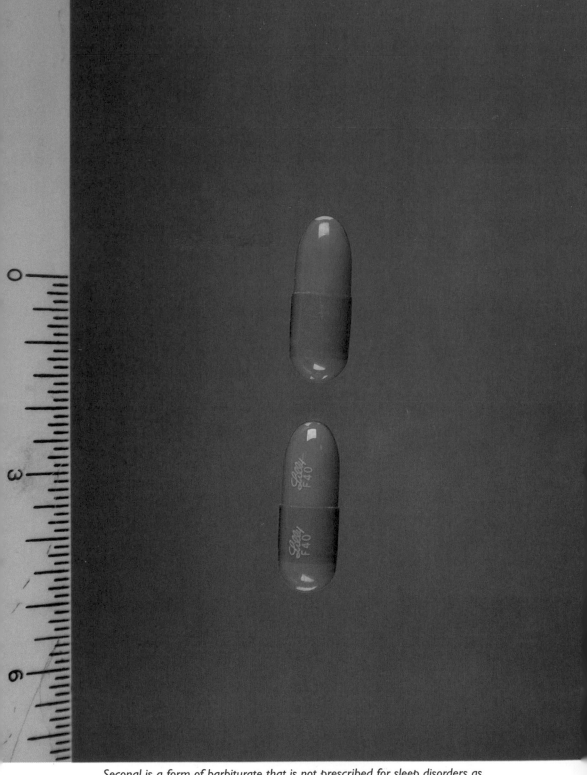

Seconal is a form of barbiturate that is not prescribed for sleep disorders as often as it once was because users develop tolerance to it, which means that it is only effective as a safe sleep aid for a couple of weeks.

to achieve the same results, which could eventually result in an overdose. Abe's doctor was hopeful, however, that a couple of weeks of sleep might successfully break Abe's cycles of insomnia. The barbiturate might not be the answer to Abe's problem—but he was willing to give it a shot.

Barbiturates like Seconal are the oldest sedative-hypnotic medications still in use today, although they are not prescribed as often as in the past. Since their discovery, more than 2,500 barbiturates have been synthesized, and at one time, fifty different ones were on the market at the same time. Today, approximately twelve are available for medicinal purposes. They can be used as hypnotics, sedatives, anticonvulsants, and in high enough dosages, as anesthesia for short surgical procedures or to sedate patients prior to longer ones.

As discussed in chapter 1, the discovery of barbiturates was prompted by the inability of barbituric acid to cross the blood–brain barrier. Unlike their predecessors, barbiturates are easily dissolved in fat and can cross this barrier with ease. And because they dissolve into the body's stored fat reserves, they can build up and reenter the bloodstream later.

How barbiturates affect the brain is not entirely clear. Many researchers believe that they bind to sodium ion channels on the neurotransmitters, thereby stopping the flow of sodium ions in the brain. Other researchers believe the primary action of barbiturates is on the neurotransmitter GABA, as described earlier in this chapter.

Barbiturates are classified by how long it takes for their effects to be produced and how long those effects last at a standard dosage. Classifications are ultrashort, short, intermediate, and long-acting.

Ultrashort-acting barbiturates begin action immediately or within forty-five seconds and last between fifteen minutes and three hours. Barbiturates used for anesthetics are usually ultrashort-acting barbiturates, and the effects are felt within one minute of intravenous (IV) administration. Thiopenthal sodium, hexobarbital, and methohexital are examples of ultrashort-acting barbiturates.

Short-acting barbiturates include secobarbital (the drug Abe used) and pentobarbital. Effects can be achieved within ten to fifteen minutes and last for two to four hours.

Amobarbital, butabarbital, and Tuinal are examples of *intermediate-acting barbiturates*. It takes fifteen to thirty minutes for their action to begin. Effects last between four and six hours.

Long-acting barbiturates take between thirty minutes and an hour to begin to work, and their effects can last between six and eight hours. Phenobarbital and barbital are examples of long-acting barbiturates.

The most often abused barbiturates are those that are intermediate- and short-acting. Long-acting barbiturates take too long before any effects are felt. The effects of ultra-short-acting barbiturates come on too quickly and are over too soon for them to be worth the effort and risk of abuse.

How the body rids itself of barbiturates varies by the type of barbiturate taken. Generally, short-acting barbiturates leave the body as **metabolites** in urine. Long-acting barbiturates are generally excreted unchanged.

Benzodiazepines

The website created by the manufactures of the drug Xanax includes the real-life story of Alexandra, a twenty-seven-year-old woman:

> I just felt real dizzy, my vision was real blurred, and I couldn't catch my breath. And basically [I]

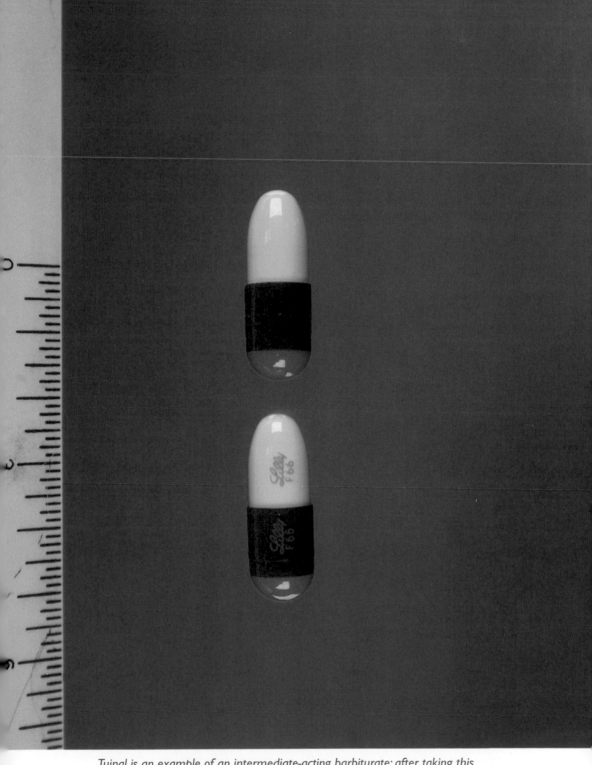

Tuinal is an example of an intermediate-acting barbiturate; after taking this medication, effects will begin to be experienced in fifteen to thirty minutes, and they will last between four and six hours.

Sedatives and Hypnotics—Deadly Downers 39

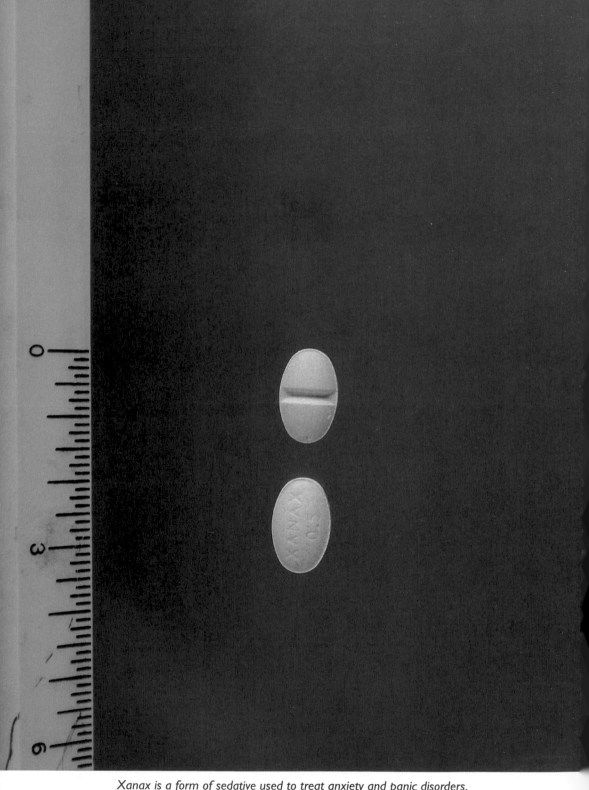

Xanax is a form of sedative used to treat anxiety and panic disorders.

didn't know what was going on with me. Well, I was a very outgoing person. I was very fun. I mean, I did everything. I wasn't afraid of anything. I traveled, I knew how to play hard and have fun, and really was fearless. I mean, I wasn't afraid to try anything—at least once.

Well, I just felt kind of unreal and not in control. My biggest fear was passing out while driving. I had just had my wisdom teeth out; it was three days later, and I was driving back to Arlington in a car. I started feeling kind of funny at first, and then I felt like I was going to pass out. My heart was racing, and I thought, "something's happening." I really thought it was related to getting my teeth out. I thought, "Maybe I tried to drive too soon." I made it back to a friend's house and called for help from there.

I was afraid to do anything at that point. I was afraid to go out—I was afraid to stay in. I was afraid to ride in a car. But my biggest fear was being alone. My life changed substantially in that I went from a carefree, outgoing, fearless person to one that was afraid of everything.

I did get an appointment with my *internist*, and they checked everything out as far as my thyroid and EKG. Everything came out normal. And that bothered me a little bit because I felt, it can't be normal—something's wrong with me. I went to a lot of specialists—*cardiologist, endocrinologist*—to keep ruling out anything physical, because I wasn't convinced even then that there wasn't. Maybe I had a [physical condition], and they just couldn't find it—and maybe that had caused it. I would have been so happy if they had found a [physical condition], because there would have been a [physical] cause.

The doctors that I went to—as far as the internist and the cardiologist and the medical doctors—they would just give me various diagnoses of anxiety and would never find anything physically wrong with me. Most of them seemed to treat it like it was stress-related—that I just needed to get a grip on things.

Alexandra felt that anxiety was not a "real" condition, the way a "physical condition" would have been—but an anxiety disorder is very real. What she is experiencing is a type of anxiety disorder called a panic disorder. This type of psychiatric disorder is characterized by unexpected and repeated episodes of intense fear accompanied by physical symptoms that may include chest pain, heart palpitations, shortness of breath, dizziness, or abdominal distress. Xanax is just one of the many sedatives called benzodiazepines that could be used to treat a panic disorder.

After their creation, it did not take long for benzodiazepines to overtake barbiturates in the pharmaceutical market. Four benzodiazepines—alprazolam (Xanax), clonazepam (Klonopin), diazepam (Valium), and lorazepam (Ativan)—are often in the top-100 of medications prescribed during a year. Fifteen benzodiazepines are currently available legally in the United States. Twenty more are available in various countries throughout the world. Benzodiazepines are used for sedation, to promote sleep, to relieve anxiety, to alleviate muscle spasms, and to prevent seizures.

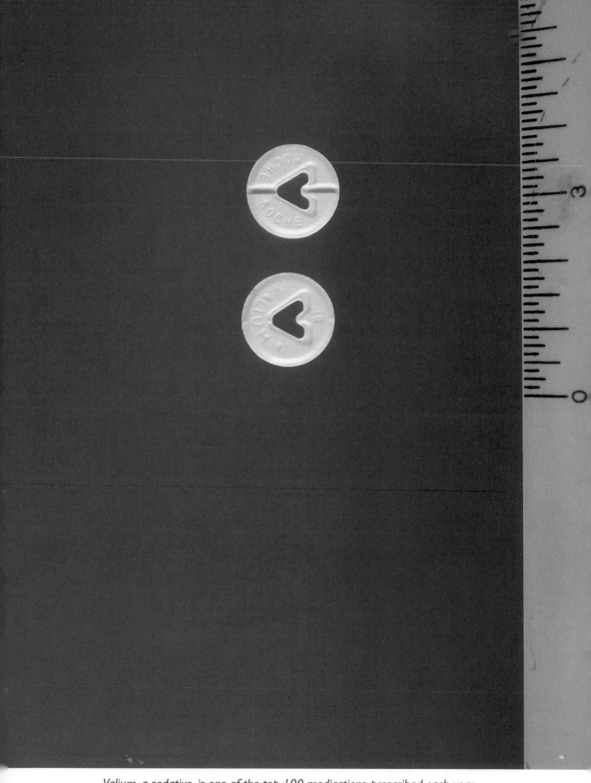

Valium, a sedative, is one of the top-100 medications prescribed each year.

Sedatives and Hypnotics—Deadly Downers 43

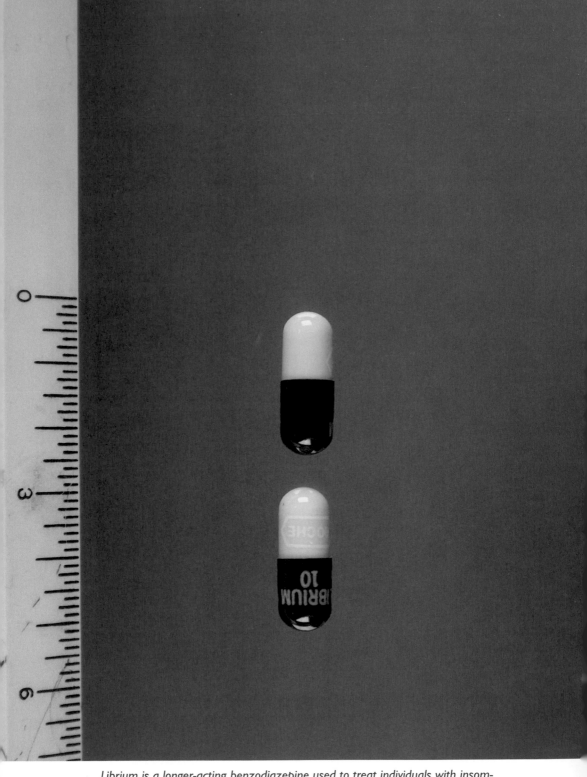

Librium is a longer-acting benzodiazepine used to treat individuals with insomnia and anxiety.

Like barbiturates, benzodiazepines work on GABA and GABA-A. They have their own binding site on the receptor, and appear to work on different subunits than barbiturates.

Benzodiazepines are categorized by how long their effects act under regular dosages. Short-acting benzodiazepines act for fewer than six hours and have few adverse effects if taken before bedtime. They are often prescribed for people suffering from difficulty in falling asleep but who do not have daytime anxiety. Some of the short-acting benzodiazepines used to treat sleep-onset insomnia include estazolam (ProSom), flurazepam (Dalmane), and triazolam (Halcion). Another short-acting benzodiazepine is Midazolam (Versed), which is used for sedation, anxiety, and amnesia in critical care settings. Longer-acting benzodiazepines are used to treat individuals with insomnia and daytime anxiety. These drugs include alprazolam (Xanax), chlordiazepoxide (Librium), and diazepam (Valium). The effects of long-lasting benzodiazepines can last for six to ten hours, and there may be some aftereffects.

Benzodiazepines can accumulate in the body. Their elimination varies greatly among individuals, and the elderly may be more strongly affected.

Side Effects

No matter how beneficial medications are, most have some potential side effects. Sometimes these potential side effects are minor; individuals taking the medication may decide that the benefits of the drug outweigh any potential side effects. In other cases, the potential side effects might be so severe and uncomfortable that an individual decides to forgo that particular medication for another one. It is important that anyone contemplating taking any medication become fully aware of not only the benefits of taking that particular drug but the downside as well. In the case of sedative-hypnotics, many of the side effects mimic those of alcohol, another CNS depressant.

Some of the potential side effects of sedative-hypnotics include:

- drowsiness, impaired judgment, and diminished motor skills even at low doses
- significant impact on driving ability, job performance, and personal relationships
- dose-related *anterograde* amnesia
- slurred speech, *ataxia*
- decreased reflex reaction
- *stupor*, coma, and *cardiorespiratory arrest* (more prevalent with barbiturates)

Rebound insomnia may be a problem for some individuals taking sedative-hypnotics for sleep issues. With rebound insomnia, symptoms return after the person stops taking the medication. These effects generally last only for a few days.

At higher dosages, sedative-hypnotics may cause lightheadedness, *vertigo*, and even anxiety, nightmares, aggression, and rage, although the latter are rare. Some people who take high doses of sedative-hypnotics find they have an altered perception of time and space and a reduced sensitivity to pain.

Besides dosage, the environment of the person taking barbiturates also influences the type of reaction. For

Sedatives can cause daytime sleepiness at times when a person needs to be alert.

Sedatives and Hypnotics—Deadly Downers

example, in a peaceful setting, someone taking a low dose of barbiturate will probably feel sleepy and may even fall asleep. But if the same person takes the identical dosage in a social setting, perhaps at a party or at dinner with friends, instead of feeling sleepy, she might begin to exhibit effects similar to those she might have when drinking an alcoholic beverage: feeling "giddy"; slurred speech; impaired motor coordination; a loss of inhibition; and unpredictable emotions—happy and laughing at one minute, tearful or even angry the next.

Higher dosages of barbiturates also result in shallow and irregular breathing. In rare cases, a high dose can cause respiratory arrest and possibly death. The possibility of this happening increases if the individual takes barbiturates along with other chemicals that depress the CNS, including alcohol, narcotics, and antihistamines. Long-term effects of high-dose barbiturates include impaired memory and judgment, hostility, depression, and mood swings. Any preexisting emotional disorders can be stimulated or

Fast Fact

Rohypnol is a dangerous drug for women, especially around college campuses, though it is available around all populations. To reduce the possibility of falling victim to the date-rape drug, a woman should never leave her drink unattended. If you get up to dance or go to the restroom, don't drink something you left at the table. And though someone offering to get you a drink might seem like a nice thing for him to do, it might not be a safe thing—for you. Get your own drink, or go with him to get it.

If a person taking a low-dose barbiturate is in a quiet setting, she may fall asleep.

Sleep Eating

Some people taking the sleep aid Ambien® noticed they were gaining weight. Weight gain wasn't one of the side effects they had been warned about, and their eating habits hadn't changed—at least as far as they knew.

In truth, however, according to anecdotal evidence, their eating habits had changed after they began taking Ambien. During the course of the night, these people were getting up and getting something to eat. Afterward, they would return to bed and continue sleeping until morning, never realizing they had made the nocturnal visits to their kitchens. Their unwanted pounds were coming from sleep eating.

exacerbated with long-term use of high-dose barbiturates.

In themselves, benzodiazepines have little respiratory depressive effects. However, many people who abuse them do so in combination with CNS depressants such as alcohol. When used together, respiratory distress can occur, and can even be fatal.

Anterograde memory loss has also been found in people taking benzodiazepines. People with this side effect have an inability to recall things after they have taken the drug. Things that have happened in the past (before taking the drug), however, they are able to recall. This type of memory loss is also found in people who abuse alcohol, when it is usually referred to as having experienced a blackout.

People who take sedative-hypnotics and who are also alcoholics have an added risk. Sedative-hypnotics enhance the effect of other drugs that work as CNS depressants. This is especially true of alcohol. In fact, most deaths today that are linked to sedative-hypnotic medications also involve the **concomitant** use of alcohol.

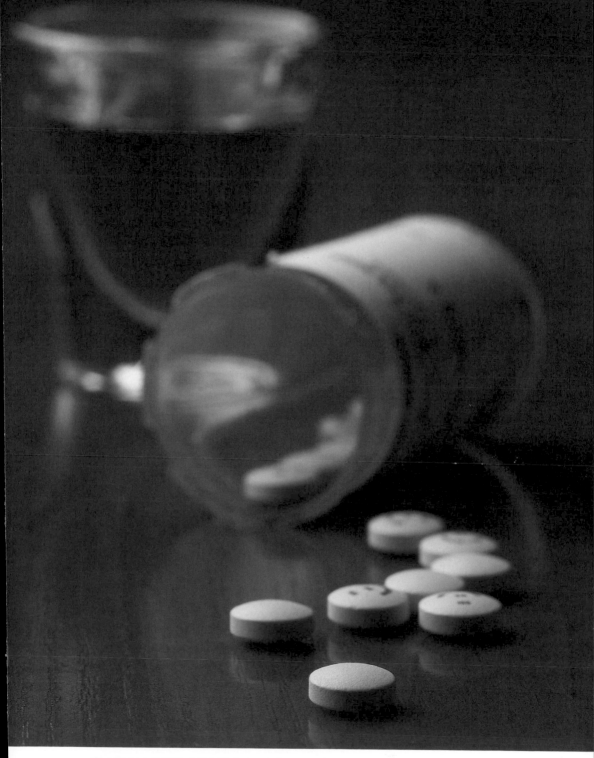

Combining alcohol and sedatives can be very dangerous. It can slow breathing down to the point that the person may die.

Sedatives and Hypnotics—Deadly Downers 51

A person who is afraid of flying might be given a one-dose treatment of a sedative-hypnotic to help him cope with his anxiety.

Cross-tolerance is also a potential side effect for *chronic* users of barbiturates. Because the effects of alcohol, minor tranquilizers, and some anesthetics are very similar, someone who has developed a tolerance to barbiturates may show evidence of tolerance with these other substances as well.

Contraindications and Other Risks

There is little argument that sedative-hypnotic drugs have successfully helped many people with sleep disorders, tension, anxiety, and other problems. However, the drugs are not a *panacea*, and not everyone should be given prescriptions for such medications. For example, many doctors believe that sedative-hypnotics should not be prescribed to people with substance abuse problems unless their success in the *detoxification* process has been shown previously or in the case of a one-dose *protocol* for a panic disorder (for example, to allow someone afraid of flying to take a necessary trip).

Studies have linked sedative-hypnotic drugs with birth defects and behavioral problems in babies and children. Infants whose mothers were taking sedative-hypnotics were also reported to suffer from more breathing difficulties than those whose mothers were not on the medications. In addition, affected babies have been reported to suffer from difficulty feeding, sleep disorders, sweating, irritability, and fever. As with babies born to mothers on other medications or illegal drugs, some babies have shown sedative-hypnotic drug withdrawal symptoms at birth.

Other health risks include:

- anemia
- impaired liver function

- headache, blurred vision, and slurred speech indicative of intoxication
- depression
- decreased ability of the body to absorb vitamins D and K (especially from barbiturate use)

Barbiturates can seriously affect the ability of other medications to do their jobs. For example, oral corticosteroids, *estrogen*, oral contraceptives, blood-thinning medications, and some antibiotics and anticonvulsants may not be as effective when combined with barbiturates.

Another risk some experts associate with sedative-hypnotics use is called drug automatism. Experts have not reached a **consensus** as to whether this condition actually exists, but growing evidence indicates there is something to the concept. In drug automatism, someone who is under the influence of a sedative-hypnotic—and who may be in a confused state—is unaware that he has taken a dose of medication. So he takes another dose. This often leads to a fatal overdose.

When a person stops taking sedative-hypnotics, he faces another set of risks. These are serious, and can even be life-threatening. According to the U.S. Drug Enforcement Administration (DEA), barbiturate withdrawal symptoms include:

- anxiety
- insomnia
- seizures
- nausea and other stomach-related problems
- hallucinations

Barbiturates can make oral contraceptives less effective.

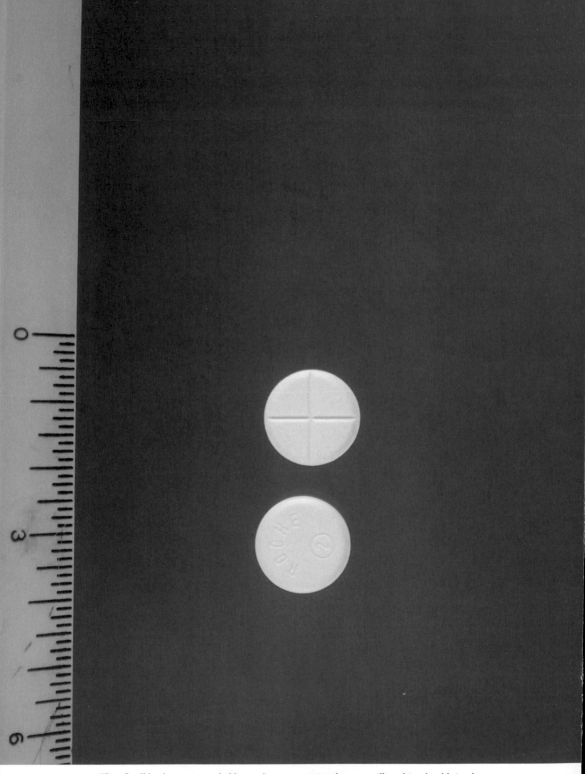

"Roofies" look very much like ordinary aspirin; they are illegal in the United States and Canada, but they are still available illegally.

The DEA cites the following as some of the symptoms of benzodiazepine withdrawal:

- anxiety
- insomnia
- tremors
- delirium
- convulsions
- death
- abdominal pain
- agitation
- dizziness
- flu-like symptoms
- *agoraphobia*
- depression
- irrational fear and paranoia
- rapid mood changes

There is no such thing as a symptom-free withdrawal from sedative-hypnotics. It should only be done under the supervision of a qualified health-care professional. Individuals going through withdrawal should realize that it is a process, and it can be a painful one at that. (Withdrawal and treatment are covered in depth later in this book.)

Not all risks involve one's health in the same way as those listed previously. One of the benzodiazepines—Rohypnol—has gained an infamous reputation as a tool in sexual assaults. Roofies, or rophies, the "date-rape drug," makes the recipient's muscles relax and produces anterograde memory loss. The drug is usually unknowingly slipped into a drink, and after the drug's effects have gone into action, the woman is sexually assaulted. When the

At parties, make a practice of getting your own drinks; never leave your drink unattended.

effects wear off, the woman has no recollection of what happened after taking the drink. Although Rohypnol is illegal in the United States, Canada, and many other countries, it continues to be available illegally, and it has become a growing problem for law enforcement.

Perhaps sedative-hypnotics' most serious risks—and potential side effects—are tolerance and dependence.

3 Getting Hooked: Misuse and Abuse

A recent article on the BBC website tells the story of Susan Hyatt, who three years ago was prescribed a benzodiazepine for anxiety. She has been slowly coming off the drug over the last twelve months, but every time she cuts down, her symptoms are worse than the original anxiety. She told the BBC interviewer: "I have physical symptoms which are the palpitations, hot and cold sweats, shaking, trembling to the psychological symptoms which is I think that I am going to lose it, I think I am going crazy."

The BBC reports that tales of tranquilizer addiction are nothing new. For the past twenty-five years, users have reported numerous stories of addiction. Around the world, doctors have been warned that benzodiazepines should not be prescribed for longer than four weeks, that they should be given in the lowest possible doses, and that they should not be used to treat depression. And yet addictions continue to exist.

Without a doubt, sedative-hypnotics have allowed many individuals to lead what most would claim to be more "normal" lives. For them, the route to the drugs came through legitimate prescriptions written by health-care professionals. But not everyone who takes sedative-hypnotics does so because of a medical condition.

Who Is Abusing Sedative-Hypnotics?

The National Survey on Drug Use and Health (NSDUH) has reported an alarming increase in the nonmedical use of prescription drugs during the past few years. The NSDUH defines nonmedical use as occurring when an individual takes prescription medications that were not prescribed for her, or who takes the medication only for the feeling that results from taking it. Although sedative-hypnotics are one of the least used drugs taken nonmedically, the statistics are still relevant. According to the NSDUH study, in 2010:

Fast Fact

The use of sedative-hypnotic medications is more prevalent in whites than in any other race.

- 2.2 million and 374,000 individuals admitted to the nonmedical use of tranquilizers and sedatives, respectively.
- 1.2 million and 252,000 individuals admitted they had used tranquilizers and sedatives, respectively, for nonmedical purposes for the first time during the previous year.

Canadians and Tranquilizers

According to Canadian author Janet C. Currie, who wrote *Manufacturing Addiction: The Over-Prescription of Tranquilizers and Sleeping Pills to Women in Canada*, the overprescription of benzodiazepines (tranquilizers) to women in Canada was first identified as a critical health-care issue in the 1970s. Despite this realization thirty years earlier, Currie points out that in the year 2000 alone, Canadian retail pharmacies filled for women more than 15.7 million prescriptions for tranquilizers. When women go to their doctor with similar symptoms as men, they are more likely than men to be prescribed benzodiazepines. According to Currie, physicians prescribe benzodiazepines and sleeping pills to help women cope with work or family stress, premenstrual syndrome, grief, and adjustment to life events such as childbirth and menopause, or for chronic illness and pain. Nondrug treatments for these circumstances and conditions continue to be underpromoted and underused. What's more, one in every three Aboriginal (North American Indian) women over forty in Western Canada was prescribed tranquilizers or sleeping pills in 2000. Aboriginal women are also almost twice as likely to receive tranquilizer prescriptions as Aboriginal men. Meanwhile, as many as 50 percent of all women over sixty in Canada may be prescribed tranquilizers or sleeping pills. Long-term care facilities, which have a higher proportion of female residents than male, also have high levels of benzodiazepine prescription rates. These drugs are a common cause of confusion, cognitive decline, and dementia in elders. Long-term tranquilizer use has also been linked to an increased risk of falls and hip and femur fractures among the elderly. British Columbia's Provincial Health Officer, Dr. Perry Kendall, states that among the poor, benzodiazepines may be used to numb patients to the physical and mental pain of poverty and harsh reality.

Currie recommends that nondrug treatments and resources, currently underpromoted and underused, be further explored. Health Canada (the Canadian federal health-care program) and the provincial/territorial governments should provide funding and support to community-based organizations to explore and provide free of charge nondrug advice and options that support women's well-being and help women cope with life's challenges. By allowing the overprescription and inappropriate use of benzodiazepines and sleeping pills to women in Canada, Currie, states, Canadians are "manufacturing addiction" and contributing to escalating health-care costs. She believes that action to address this problem is long overdue.

An alarming number of people, especially young people, use sedatives for nonmedical uses.

Among individuals between the ages of twelve and seventeen, 3.2 percent reported using tranquilizers at some time during their lives; in 2009 1 percent reported using sedatives during that period. When surveyed about nonmedical use of tranquilizers and sedatives during the past year, the numbers were 2.1 percent and 0.5 percent, respectively. Less than one percent admitted to using tranquilizers or sedatives during the previous thirty days.

As the ages surveyed increase, so does the nonmedical use of these drugs. The 2010 NSDUH study found that the average age of initial use for tranquilizers was 24.6; for sedatives it was 23.5. Although some teenagers are using these drugs, it tends to be the drug of choice for a slightly older crowd.

The nonmedical use of sedative-hypnotics reflects an alarming trend in drug use: the nonmedical use of prescription medications. In fact, most teenage survey participants indicated that they used prescription medication as their drug of choice because it was easily obtainable; after all, prescription medications can be found in the medicine cabinets in many homes. A study conducted by the National Institute on Drug Abuse (NIDA) in 2004 found that, in some areas, teens would gather up old prescription medications, get together with other teens at "pharming parties," and trade for other prescription drugs. At some parties, teens bring whatever prescription drugs they find in their medicine cabinets, throw them all into a bowl, and pass it around, taking whatever they want; this is the "salad bowl." Many Internet sites also offer prescription sedative-hypnotic drugs, some advertising that a prescription is not needed. A Google search in March, 2012, for "no prescription needed Valium" returned almost 1.5

Teens who misuse sedatives sometimes mix them with other drugs, which can increase their danger.

Express Scripts, Inc., a managed-care pharmacy, surveyed more than 13,000 women sixty years old and older who had been prescribed benzodiazepines. According to their study, more than 50 percent were taking the medications improperly. Almost 60 percent had been taking the benzodiazepines for four or more months, significantly increasing their likelihood of developing a dependence or addiction.

million hits. Although businesses may advertise that prescriptions are not necessary, it is illegal to purchase *controlled substances* without one.

Another reason teens are turning to prescription medications, including sedative-hypnotics, is that they consider them to be safer than street drugs; just under 50 percent of those surveyed did not see a major risk in taking prescription medications. After all, these medications were prescribed by a physician or other health-care professional permitted by law to do so. If the medications were available for dispensing, teens reason, these drugs had to have been approved by the FDA in the United States or the Therapeutic Product Directorate in Canada. What some teens fail to realize, however, is that the medications are approved for use for a specific purpose (and that purpose is not getting high) under the direction of a health-care professional. Advertising on television and in other media have made the teenage abuser well educated about the brand names and effects caused by many of these prescription medications.

Individuals who use illegal drugs often use sedative-hypnotics, especially barbiturates. People who use heroin often mix it and barbiturates to get a more intense high. Since both barbiturates and heroin depress respiration, this can be an extremely dangerous practice. Methamphetamine users also combine their drug of choice with barbiturates; when someone who uses meth often over a course of several days, severe hyperactivity can result—and to counteract the telltale hyperactivity, some meth users will take sedative-hypnotics.

How Addiction Develops

After taking some medications, including sedative-hypnotics, for a period of time, the body often builds up a tolerance toward the drug. To achieve the same results that were received when the individual first started taking the drug, higher doses must be taken, sometimes at more-frequent intervals. In the case of sedative-hypnotics, tolerance can build up relatively quickly. The level of tolerance—and how quickly that level develops—depends on the dose, frequency of administration, and the individual person, including one's metabolism; not everyone will develop a tolerance at the same point in their use history. When someone stops taking the drug, she experiences withdrawal symptoms because her body has become dependent on the medication. By following the instructions of the health-care professional, dependence can be treated and withdrawal symptoms minimized and possibly eliminated with proper dosage adjustments.

Sometimes the need for the drug is more than physical. If an individual must take the drug to satisfy emotional and psychological needs, he has developed an addiction to the substance. A person addicted to the drug has a *compulsive* need to use the medication for non-medical purposes. His behavior can become *erratic* and include stealing drugs from friends and family members and selling and buying drugs on the street.

In the case of sedative-hypnotics, as with the misuse and abuse of many prescription medications, nonmedi-

Abuse or Misuse?

Abuse and misuse are two different things; unfortunately, both can lead to addiction.

Misuse:

Patients may forget or not understand their prescription's directions. They may start making their own decisions, perhaps upping the dose in hopes of getting better faster.

Abuse:

People may use prescription drugs for nonmedical reasons. Prescription drug abusers may obtain such drugs illegally and use them to get high, fight stress, or boost energy.

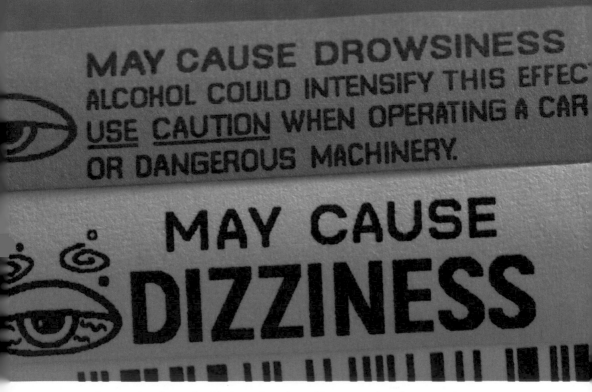

Prescription drugs should always be taken with care, paying close attention to all label warnings.

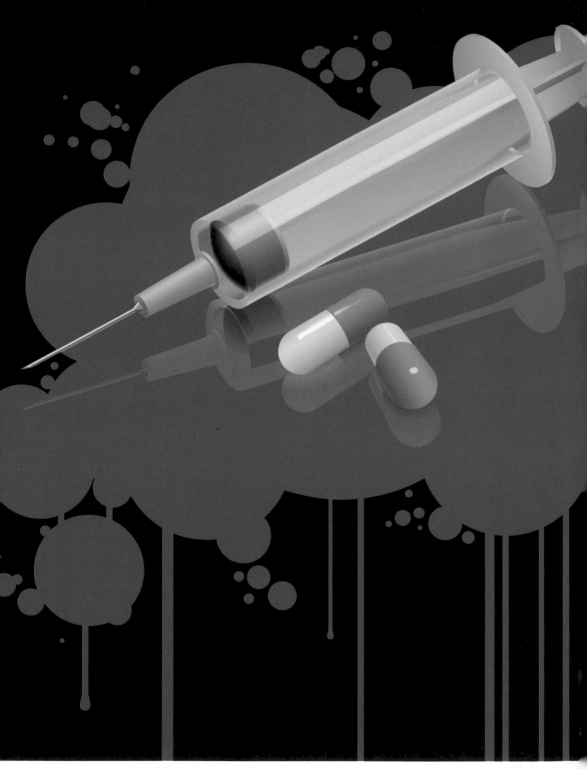

Heroin and benzodiazepines are a deadly combination.

cal use generally be-
gins with a medically
prescribed dosage. As
the body builds toler-
ance, the individual in-
creases the dosage until
it is often several times
the prescribed amount.
With barbiturates, this
is particularly danger-

Fast Fact

All sedative-hypnotics can be
abused. There is no such thing
as a completely safe sedative-
hypnotic.

ous. Though the body becomes tolerant to the "high"
created by the drugs, it does not develop a tolerance to
its life-threatening effects. As a result, the person who
has a tolerance to barbiturates can ingest a fatal overdose
and never feel the high.

Abuse of benzodiazepines can also have fatal results
when combined with alcohol or other depressants. Individuals who abuse heroin and cocaine are also frequent
abusers of benzodiazepines. According to the DEA, an
estimated 50 percent of people who undergo treatment
for narcotic or cocaine addiction report abusing benzodiazepines as well.

Long-term use of benzodiazepines usually leads to some
degree of tolerance or dependence; that seems to be the
nature of the drug. Most treatment protocols call for their
use to be limited to two to four weeks, which includes a
period of *taper dosing*. Tolerance to benzodiazepines can
create a range of side effects that can be worse than the
condition for which they were first prescribed. Tolerance
to the hypnotic effects of benzodiazepines often occurs
within only a few days. Symptoms of benzodiazepine tolerance can mimic those of the drug's withdrawal and include
abdominal pain, tremors, depression, and rapid mood
change. (A more complete list is provided in chapter 2.)

If a person is addicted to sedative-hypnotics, his thoughts are consumed with thinking about when he can use the drug again.

It is important to remember that under medical care, these are legal medications with legitimate medical indications. But, when someone becomes addicted, she may feel the need to do whatever she can to get the medication. The addicted person may begin to lie, obsessively count the pills, steal prescription pads, forge doctors' signatures, and "doctor shop" by going to different doctors to get prescriptions for the medications. He may return to his health-care provider and tell her that he "lost" his medication, that it fell into the toilet, or even that his dog ate it—all with the goal of getting more of the drug.

To the person who has developed an addiction to sedative-hypnotics, the purpose of life becomes focused on thinking about, getting, and using more of the drug. Some seem to be content with this all-consuming life pattern. Others, however, find themselves—some by choice, others not—in treatment programs with the goal of getting their lives back from the clutches of drug misuse and abuse.

4 Getting Help: Kicking the Habit

His is one of the most famous last names in U.S. politics. But, in the spring of 2006, Patrick Kennedy was in the news for another, less favorable, reason—a car accident, an antihistamine taken for pain, and Ambien. According to a story in the *Washington Times*:

> Rep. Patrick J. Kennedy yesterday blamed his early-morning car crash on a "chronic" addiction to pain pills before announcing he is re-entering drug rehabilitation at the Mayo Clinic, his third treatment since Christmas.
>
> The Rhode Island Democrat and son of Democratic Sen. Edward M. Kennedy of Massachusetts said he didn't remember driving into a security

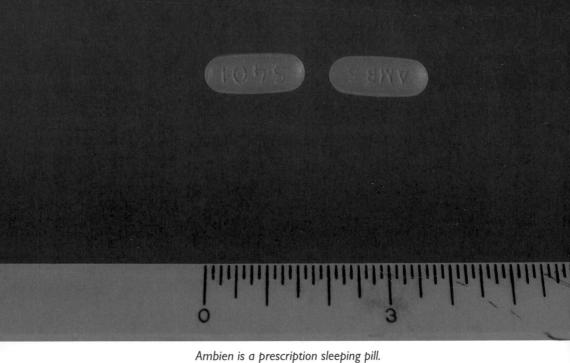

Ambien is a prescription sleeping pill.

barrier near the Capitol Thursday, but that he had taken Phenergan, a sedative for stomach pain, and Ambien, a sleeping pill.

"I simply do not remember getting out of bed, being pulled over by the police, or being cited for three driving infractions," Mr. Kennedy, 38, said during a brief press conference.

Asked if he will resign, Mr. Kennedy responded: "No, I need to stay in the fight."

The police report says Mr. Kennedy's "eyes were red and watery, speech was slightly slurred, and upon exiting his vehicle, his balance was unsure." When questioned about the 2:45 a.m. Thursday accident, Mr. Kennedy said he was "headed to the Capitol to make a vote," the report said.

The congressman said he admitted himself to the Mayo Clinic in Rochester, Minn., at Christmas and later during an unspecified House recess for addiction to prescription pain medicine. In his younger years, Mr. Kennedy was treated for cocaine abuse.

"I've been fighting this chronic disease since I was a young man and have aggressively and periodically sought treatment so that I can live a full and productive life," said Mr. Kennedy, who has been open about being diagnosed with bipolar disorder.

He also said: "The reoccurrence of an addiction problem can be triggered by things that happen in everyday life, such as taking a common treatment for a stomach flu. That's not an excuse for what happened Wednesday evening, but it is a reality of fighting a chronic condition for which I'm taking full responsibility."

Patrick Kennedy's story is not unlike many heard before. It reflects the fact that addiction to any substance is an ongoing battle. There are no quick fixes, and relapses are not uncommon. And, it's not an easy process, as the story of a fifty-one-year-old physician told in a 2002 *Chicago Tribune* article confirms:

For the 51-year-old physician reducing the dose of Xanax was physically painful. His anxiety clawed back, he couldn't sleep and a million butterflies seemed to churn in his stomach, disturbing sensations he now recognizes as withdrawal symptoms.

He became both chemically dependent on Xanax and psychologically addicted to it.

He chased the ever-fleeting "normal" feeling by taking more Xanax and drinking more alcohol. For four years his life descended deeper and deeper into addiction.

"That's when I really started doing some suicidal thinking," he said. "Not that I would ever carry it out, but I really began for the first time in my life to have some concrete plans for how I would end my life."

Sedative abuse plus driving often equals an accident.

Several months ago his wife staged a confrontation in the office of his psychiatrist, who by this time knew his patient was out of control. Faced with a breakup of his marriage and the loss of his medical license, he agreed to go into treatment.

He consulted an addiction specialist. "He told me that I was an addict, that I'd become addicted to Xanax. Part of that whole thing was my addictive personality, but it was also misprescribing on the part of my psychiatrist."

The physician traveled to Des Plaines where he spent a week in Holy Family Hospital's detox unit to clear Xanax from his brain.

Safely down from Xanax, he transferred to Rush-Presbyterian-St. Luke's Medical Center where he completed a 9-week program in August.

"My anxiety is under much better control," the doctor said. "I'm on no Xanax. I feel no desire to take Xanax ever again. It's a dangerous drug."

As both stories show, the first step in overcoming addiction to sedative-hypnotics is the same as with every other form of addiction: admit there is a problem, that one is an addict. For Representative Kennedy, his admission came as a result of a very public traffic accident. For the doctor, it took an *intervention* to get him to face what he already knew—he had a drug problem. In some ways, this may be one of the hardest of a series of incredibly hard steps. Treatment for sedative-hypnotic addiction can take months, even years, and it is hard work. But it is impossible to finish the journey to sobriety without taking that first step of admitting to being an addict.

Diagnosing a Drug Problem

The Diagnostic and Statistical Manual of Mental Disorders (DSM), published by the American Psychiatric Association, is a handbook for diagnosing psychiatric disorders. It is now in its fourth edition (IV-TR). It contains established criteria to be used in determining whether someone has a mental health condition.

DSM-IV-TR Diagnostic Criteria for Substance Abuse

Have any of the following occurred within a 12-month period?

1. Has recurrent substance use resulted in a failure to fulfill major role obligations at work, school, or home?
2. Has the patient used substances in which it is physically dangerous? (for example, driving while intoxicated)
3. Has the patient had any recurrent legal problem due to the substance use?
4. Has the patient continued to use substances despite having persistent social or interpersonal problems caused by the substance use?

DSM-IV-TR Diagnostic Criteria for Substance Dependence

Have three of more of the following occurred at any time in the same 12-month period?

1. Is the patient tolerant to the substance?
2. Is the patient in withdrawal?
3. Has the substance been taken in larger amounts or over longer periods of time than was intended?
4. Has there been a persistent desire or unsuccessful effort to cut down or control the use of the substance?
5. Is a great deal of time being spent in obtaining the substance or recovering from its use?
6. Have important social, occupational, or recreational activities been given up or reduced because of substance abuse?
7. Has the use of the substance continued despite knowledge of having recurrent or persistent physical or psychological problems that are caused or made worse by the substance abuse?

Detoxification

When one decides to break free from addiction, the body must go through a process of withdrawal to rid itself of the toxic substances of the drug. Withdrawal can be painful and, in some cases, even be life-threatening. Symptoms can range from mild (such as insomnia or loss of appetite) to moderate (tremors or muscle aches) to the severe (decreased body temperature, seizures). One should never abruptly stop taking sedative-hypnotics on their own. For individuals taking prescription sedative-hypnotics, the guidance of a health-care professional, who will generally suggest a gradual weaning from the drug through increasingly smaller dosages, can prevent or lessen withdrawal symptoms; the physical toll on the body is not as extreme as it could be. Through a medically supervised process called detoxification, the individual goes through some or all of the withdrawal symptoms. How long withdrawal lasts depends on how much and what type of drug was taken.

Where detoxification takes place depends on various factors. The DSM-IV-TR indicates that the individual

Sedative-Hypnotic Withdrawal Symptoms

Mild	Moderate	Severe
Anxiety	Panic	Decreased body temperature
Insomnia	Decreased concentration	Vital sign instability
Dizziness	Tremor	Muscle fasciculations
Headache	Sweating	Seizures
Loss of appetite	Palpitations	Delirium
Increased perception of sound	Perceptual distortions	Psychosis
Irritability	Muscle aches	
Agitation	Gastrointestinal upset	
	Insomnia	
	Elevated vital signs	
	Depression	

Source: Substance Abuse and Dependence. City of Philadelphia, 2000.

You don't have to take medication to relieve tension. Petting an animal can also lower blood pressure and decrease other physical symptoms of stress.

Stress

Stress is a double-edged sword when it comes to drug abuse. For some individuals, they began using drugs—including prescription medications—to combat the effects of stress. Some studies indicate increasing stress levels in today's world may be one of the causes of increasing drug use. Now, some are addicted to the medications, bringing with it a whole new set of stressors— how to get more drugs, how to get off drugs, how to live without drugs.

In some cases, the answer to the original stress problem is to find non-drug ways of coping with it. Natural and herbal stress remedies are available, but many come with their own set of problems. Some people find physical activity such as walking, running, swimming, dancing, or yoga to be effective stress relievers. For centuries people have practiced various meditation techniques for a variety of reasons, including stress reduction. Even knitting and petting a cat or dog can help alleviate stress.

should be admitted to a hospital for detoxification if any of the following can be answered with yes:

1. Is the patient unable to cease substance use outside of a secure, inpatient environment?
2. Is the patient in danger of serious withdrawal symptoms?
3. Does the patient have a physical disorder that will complicate the treatment of the patient?
4. Is the patient a danger to self or others?
5. Is the patient incapable of meeting basic needs?

For most people addicted to prescription medications such as sedative-hypnotics, the detoxification process is just a first step. In some cases, it might be all that is needed to prevent further misuse. For almost all, including those addicted to sedative-hypnotics, follow-up treatment is necessary to prevent further misuse and

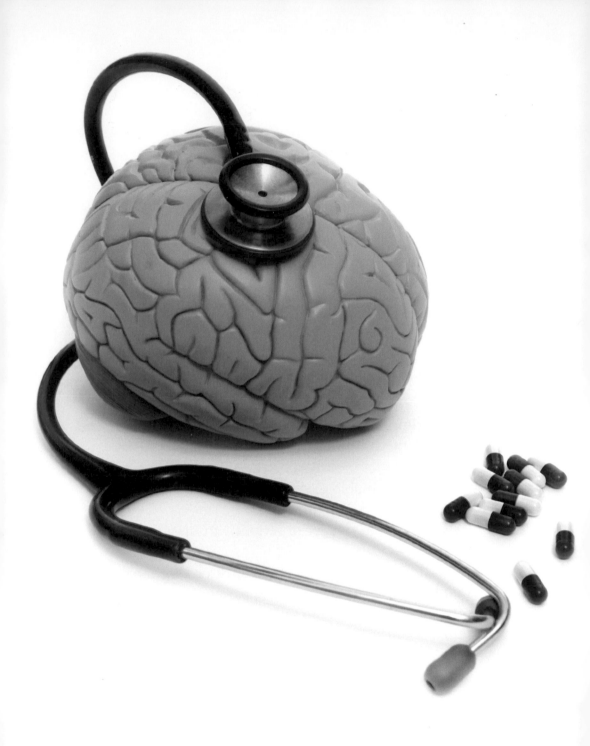

Mental health is a complicated goal that often requires a combination of medical and psychological intervention.

abuse. Studies have shown that the prognosis for individuals who abuse sedative-hypnotics is guarded; some research has found that more than 80 percent return to their abusing behaviors within four to six years after leaving treatment. Follow-up care increases the possibility that treatment will have long-term success. The most effective method of treating sedative-hypnotic addiction is behavioral therapy.

Behavioral Treatment Programs

Put simply, behavioral treatment programs teach people with addictions to change their behaviors so they are less likely to repeat those that led to addiction in the first place. Unfortunately, nothing about addiction is simple. Though behavioral treatment programs do help those with addictions find ways to avoid behaviors that can cause a relapse, they also need to help them discover what led to those behaviors initially. Individual and family therapy can help the person with addiction and those around her learn how to live with and as a recovering addict. Therapy can also help the addicted individual and her associates handle relapses; most people do relapse at some point during recovery.

Behavioral treatment programs also help those with addictions handle life without the sedative-hypnotic. If the individual began using a sedative-hypnotic for a true medical need, she will have to learn how to deal with that condition should it persist. This can mean learning new, alternative methods of treatment. These can include exercise, nutrition, and relaxation methods. Everyone associated with treatment should keep in mind that the best results are achieved when the individual practices *abstinence* from sedative-hypnotics.

Inpatient programs for drug abuse allow medical personnel to focus on a patient's issues.

DSM Discharge from Rehabilitation Services Criteria

Yes to 1–5 for a therapeutic discharge

1. Has the patient developed the skills needed to address relapse triggers in a positive manner?
2. Has the patient accepted the diagnosis of addiction and recognized its severity?
3. Is the patient able to maintain therapeutic gains in a less structured treatment setting?
4. Is the patient prepared to cope with a return to a home environment?
5. Has the patient sufficiently improved cognitively, emotionally, and physically to be able to benefit from therapy at a lower level of care?

Sufficient for discharge: Yes to 6, 7, 8, or 9

6. Has the patient's progress plateaued and is continued care at this level unlikely to achieve a significant change in the patient's status in a reasonable length of time?
7. Is the patient being retained in a rehab setting solely for the purpose of awaiting housing placement?
8. Is the patient failing to comply with the expected requirements of the residential treatment setting?
9. Has the patient had a UDS [urine drug screen] indicating use of drugs or alcohol during the stay at the rehabilitation setting?

Behavioral treatment programs often begin with a period of inpatient treatment. Depending on the length, severity, and drug of addiction, inpatient treatment can be short-term (usually a minimum of thirty days) or long-term residential. At first, some programs allow inpatients to have minimal—if any—contact with the "outside world." They concentrate on learning about themselves and their relationship with the drug. Later, family and

Cognitive-behavioral therapy helps patients learn new thought habits.

perhaps close friends are encouraged to participate in the treatment program.

Cognitive-Behavioral Therapy

A cognitive-behavioral approach to treatment encourages users to identify thought patterns and habits that have contributed to their habits. With this type of treatment, individuals learn how to change negative thought patterns, thereby changing behaviors. This is a short-term, focused approach to helping addicted individuals become abstinent from drugs. The underlying assumption is that learning processes play an important role in the development and continuation of drug abuse and dependence.

The same learning processes can be employed to help individuals reduce drug use. This approach attempts to help patients to recognize, avoid, and cope; for example, recognize the situations in which they are most likely to use sedatives, avoid these situations when appropriate, and cope more effectively with a range of problems and behaviors associated with drug abuse. Patients are encouraged to specifically identify these triggers and to restructure their lifestyles to avoid them.

Complicating Factors to Treatment

A major factor complicating treatment for sedative-hypnotic addiction is polydrug abuse. As mentioned elsewhere in this book, many sedative-hypnotics abusers have addictions to other drugs as well. This coaddiction puts a multitude of stumbling blocks on the pathway to sobriety. Not only does the addiction to the sedative-hypnotic have to be dealt with, so does the addiction to the other substance. This can mean a more difficult and much longer treatment time.

Coaddiction also increases the possibility of relapse. Most individuals undergoing drug treatment relapse; that is an unfortunate fact of rehabilitation. Health-care professionals, family, friends, and the individual must all be aware of that fact. And they must also be aware that with a dependence on more than one substance, relapse is even more likely. This is particularly true if the person is addicted to a legal substance such as alcohol. Also complicating recovery is another fact: sedative-hypnotics are sometimes given in the treatment process for addictions to other substances, including alcohol. When treating coaddiction, total honesty about the addiction—or addictions—between the individual and the health-care provider is an absolute necessity. Success can depend on it.

In addition to formal behavioral treatment programs, individuals are also encouraged to supplement their programs with support groups such as Narcotics Anonymous (NA). When begun within the inpatient treatment setting, programs such as NA can help ease transition into the "real world," where the individual is once again faced with daily temptations.

Narcotics Anonymous

Based on the twelve-step program of Alcoholics Anonymous (AA), Narcotics Anonymous (NA) helps those addicted to sedative-hypnotics and other drugs to stay sober in the outside world. Not all individuals who take advantage of what NA has to offer have been in rehab programs. Some use NA to kick drug habits on their own, though that is definitely not the way to go with sedative-hypnotics addiction. The first NA meetings were held in the early 1950s in Los Angeles, California. As found on its website (www.na.org), the organization described itself this way in its first publication:

> NA is a nonprofit fellowship or society of men and women for whom drugs had become a major problem. We . . . meet regularly to help each other stay

Alcoholics Anonymous' logo indicates Narcotics Anonymous' same foundation of principles.

clean. . . . We are *not* interested in what or how much you used . . . but only in what you want to do about your problem and how we can help.

In the more than fifty years since, NA has grown into one of the largest organizations of its kind. Today, groups

The Twelve Steps encourage those with addictions to reach up to a "Higher Power" for help.

are located all over the world, and its books and pamphlets are published in thirty-two languages. No matter where the group is located, each chapter is based on the twelve steps first formulated in AA:

1. We admitted we were powerless over drugs—that our lives had become unmanageable.
2. Came to believe that a Power greater than ourselves could restore us to sanity.
3. Made a decision to turn our will and our lives over to the care of God as we understand Him.
4. Made a searching and fearless moral inventory of ourselves.
5. Admitted to God, and to our selves, and to another human being the exact nature of our wrongs.
6. We're entirely ready to have God remove all these defects of character.
7. Humbly asked Him to remove our shortcomings.
8. Made a list of all persons we had harmed, and became willing to make amends to them all.
9. Made direct amends to such people wherever possible, except when to do so would injure them or others.
10. Continued to take personal inventory and when we were wrong promptly admitted it.
11. Sought through prayer and meditation to improve our conscious contact with God as we understand Him, praying only for knowledge of His will for us and the power to carry that out.
12. Having had a spiritual awakening as the result of these steps, we tried to carry this message to drug addicts and to practice these principles in all our affairs.

Although many cities have NA groups, individuals going through drug recovery can feel at home at AA

What Do Rehab Programs Accomplish?

Abstinence

In many cases it seems that as long as the substance is in the blood stream, thinking remains distorted. Often during the first days or weeks of total abstinence, we see a gradual clearing of thinking processes. This is a complex psychological and biological phenomenon, and is one of the elements that inpatient programs are able to provide by making sure the patient is fully detoxified and remains abstinent during his or her stay.

Removal of Denial

In some cases, when someone other than the patient, such as a parent, employer, or other authority, is convinced there is a problem, but the addict is not yet sure, voluntary attendance at a rehab program will provide enough clarification to remove this basic denial. Even those who are convinced they have a problem with substances usually don't admit to themselves or others the full extent of the addiction. Rehab uses group process to identify and help the individual to let go of these expectable forms of denial.

Removal of Isolation

As addictions progress, relationships deteriorate in quality. However, the bonds between fellow recovering people are widely recognized as one of the few forces powerful enough to keep recovery on track. The rehab experience, whether it is inpatient or outpatient involves in-depth sharing in a group setting. This kind of sharing creates strong interpersonal bonds among group members. These bonds help to form a support system that will be powerful enough to sustain the individual during the first months of abstinence.

"Basic Training"

Basic training is a good way to think of the experience of rehab. Soldiers need a rapid course to give them the basic knowledge and skills they will need to fight in a war. Some kinds of learning need to be practiced so well that you can do them without thinking. In addition to the learning, trainees become physically fit, and perhaps most important, form emotional bonds that help keep up morale when the going is hard.

(*Source*: Partnership for a Drug-Free America)

Support groups often play a vital role in the recovery process.

Sedatives and Hypnotics—Deadly Downers 95

meetings should NA not be available. Though attendance at and participation in NA meetings will not guarantee a recovery free from temptation and relapse, they can play an important role in staying sober. Al-Anon, a group for partners and friends of alcoholics, and Alateen, formed for children of alcoholics, can help friends and families dealing with the recovery of someone from sedative-hypnotic abuse.

Education

There's an old saying that goes "An ounce of prevention is worth a pound of cure." The thing about old sayings is that there is usually some truth to it—which is what makes it stick around long enough to become an old saying.

That saying is relevant to drug treatment; if you don't get addicted to drugs, then you won't have to suffer any of the negative consequences or go through the painful withdrawal symptoms. While that's true, preventing sedative-hypnotics abuse is not as simple as it might seem. Thanks to something called direct-to-consumer (DTC) advertising, people are inundated with television commercials and print ads telling them that this drug will cure stress and that one will help you get a good night's sleep. Before DTC advertising was allowed in the United States, representatives from pharmaceutical companies could only market their products to health-care professionals. Now, marketing and public relations persons working for drug companies can aim at the ultimate consumer—the patient. Instead of waiting for the health-care professional to recommend the proper medication, many patients walk in to the exam-

The Twelve Steps encourage those who have addictions to use prayer and meditation to increase their awareness of God as a source of emotional and spiritual strength.

x

Sedatives and Hypnotics—Deadly Downers 97

The Internet can be a great source of information—but some of what it offers is biased or incorrect.

ining room and ask the health-care professional for a specific medication, usually one they've seen on television or in a newspaper or magazine.

Education is one of the most important tools that can be used in the battle against drug abuse. And, many who ask their health-care professionals for a specific drug consider themselves to be an educated consumer. While some undoubtedly are, the majority base their information on what they've been told by the drug companies. People who are candidates for any type of medical treatment, including being prescribed sedative-hypnotics, should educate themselves about their condition and available treatments. When they are prescribed a medication or other regimen, they should find out as much as possible about the treatment. The Internet is chock-full of information, but care must be taken regarding the source of information. Many sites belong to drug manufacturers, so their objectivity could definitely be debated. Government sites are generally reliable ones for getting information about drugs.

There is an Internet e-mail list or chat group for almost anything anyone can imagine. While medication and treatment advice should not be taken as being true for everyone, these are good sites for getting information about new treatment methods, including alternative, nondrug therapy. This information can be given to health-care professionals to see if they are options for that particular individual. E-mail lists and chat groups are also good ways to "meet" others living with the same condition. Stories about how to cope can be shared. Perhaps most important, these online support groups can help individuals learn that they are not alone in their suffering. In-person support groups are very effective for some, but for an individual who is shy, uncomfortable about talking

The Internet allows individuals to share problems and receive support from each other without the embarrassment of talking face-to-face.

in groups, housebound, without transportation, or too ill to physically attend one, online groups can be a viable alternative.

Getting informed—educated—is not just the responsibility of the person with a condition requiring the use of sedative-hypnotics. Health-care professionals owe it to their patients to be up to date on the latest medications—including their potential side effects and contraindications. The information should be unbiased, not based on the influence of pharmaceutical companies. Nondrug alternatives should be explored. In-service presentations, conferences, journals, and the Internet can aid the health-care professional in keeping her skills sharp so she can provide her patients with the most effective care.

Despite efforts to prevent sedative-hypnotic addiction in the first place, it is most likely that it will continue. This is where legal efforts come into the picture.

The following twenty questions can help teens decide whether Alateen is for them.

1. Do you have a parent, close friend or relative whose drinking/drug use upsets you?

2. Do you cover up your real feelings by pretending you don't care?

3. Does it seem like every holiday is spoiled because of drinking/drug use?

4. Do you tell lies to cover up for someone else's drinking/drug use or what's happening in your home?

5. Do you stay out of the house as much as possible because you hate it there?

6. Are you afraid to upset someone for fear it will set off a drinking/drug use bout?

7. Do you feel nobody really loves or cares what happens to you?

8. Are you afraid or embarrassed to bring your friends home?

9. Do you think the drinker's/user's behavior is caused by you, other members of your family, friends, or rotten breaks in life?

10. Do you make threats such as, "If you don't stop drinking/using, I'll run away"?

11. Do you make promises about behavior such as, "I'll get better school marks, go to church or keep my room clean" in exchange for a promise that the drinking/drug use and fighting stop?

12. Do you feel that if your mom or dad loved you, she or he would stop drinking/using drugs?

13. Do you ever threaten or actually hurt yourself to scare your parents into saying, "I'm sorry," or "I love you"?

14. Do you believe no one could possibly understand how you feel?

15. Do you have money problems because of someone else's drinking/drug use?

16. Are meal times frequently delayed because of the drinker/user?

17. Have you considered calling the police because of drinking/drug use behaviors?

18. Have you refused dates out of fear or anxiety?

19. Do you think that if the drinker/user stopped drinking/using drugs, your other problems would be solved?

20. Do you ever treat people (teachers, school friends, team mates, etc.) unjustly because you are angry at someone else for drinking/using drugs too much?

If you have answered YES to some of these questions, Alateen may help you.

(*Source*: www.al-anon.alateen.org)

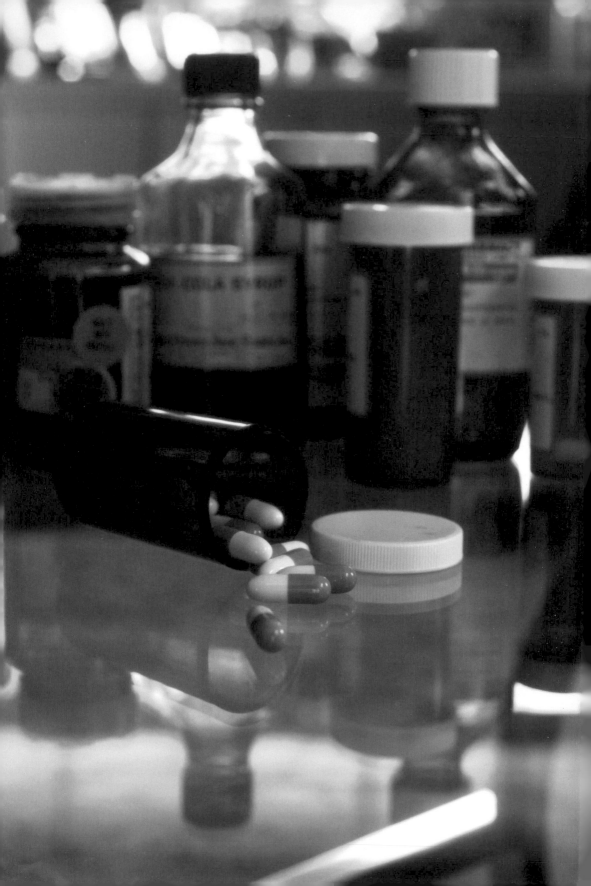

5 Legal Issues

As mentioned earlier in this book, the misuse and abuse of sedative-hypnotics is a symptom of a bigger problem in the United States, Canada, and elsewhere—the abuse of prescription medications. The legitimate medical uses for prescription medications such as sedative-hypnotics complicate law enforcement efforts in fighting drug abuse. An article in the *Washington Times* of September 2, 2003, quotes Thomas P. Lesnak, an agent with the federal Bureau of Alcohol, Tobacco, Firearms, and Explosives:

> One of the biggest problems is that when any law-enforcement officer pulls a car over and finds a prescription pill bottle in some guy's pocket, that officer ends up giving it back to the guy if it has his

name on it. Maybe that officer will write the guy a speeding ticket or whatever. If it had been a gram of cocaine valued at $100 in the guy's pocket . . . he would be in jail, with felony charges.

Though law enforcement can go after the dealers on the corner, and that does make a dent in the drug problem, many of those who fall victim to sedative-hypnotics abuse were prescribed the medication for medically legitimate reasons.

The DEA, a department within the U.S. Department of Justice, categorizes drugs according to their potential for abuse and whether they have accepted medical use. Penalties for possession and sale are partly based on where the drug falls on the DEA's Drug Schedule. Most benzodiazepines are Schedule IV drugs; in Canada, they are either Schedule F or G on Canada's Food and Drug Act.

Because of its use in criminal activities, flunitrazepam (Rohypnol) is restricted more than any other benzodiazepine in the United States and Canada. Although it is only listed as a Schedule IV drug on the DEA Drug Schedule, it cannot be purchased legally in the United States or Canada. It is the only controlled substance (except for 5 grams or more of crank), that carries a federal felony for first-offense simple possession.

In Canada, it is illegal to get a prescription for any controlled substance without first telling a physician that a similar prescription was obtained through another health-care professional within the previous thirty days. Anyone convicted of trafficking in sedative-hypnotics or possessing them for trafficking is subject to a maximum penalty of ten years in jail.

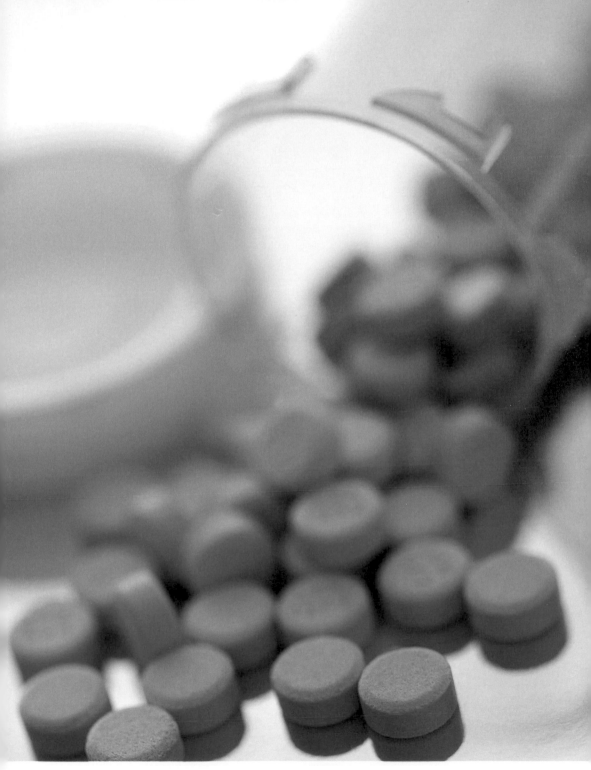

Most sedative-hypnotics are legally prescribed; when these drugs are abused, it is seldom because of dealers selling them on the streets.

U.S. and Canadian legislation is working to control the illegal buying and selling of prescription medications.

There's only so much law enforcement can do in their campaign to get illegally obtained prescription painkillers off the street.

The Legislature

As prescription medication abuse spread to the media, legislatures across the country began working to create and toughen laws pertaining to illegal buying and selling of prescription medications. In 1999, Kentucky became the first state to establish a prescription-monitoring program; 48 states now have monitoring programs. The Kentucky legislature has acted to make the program more efficient and searches more timely by approving police use of the Kentucky All Schedule Prescription Electronic Reporting System (KASPER) to track abuses by location rather than initiating a request based on a single incident. Police agencies working on regional investigations can share the information from KASPER, rather than each department filing a separate request to get the information. Pharmaceutical giant Purdue Pharma contributed funding toward the creation of a prescription-tracking program available to states.

Though buying controlled substances without a prescription is a federal offense, it is a law that is difficult to enforce when it comes to Internet sales. Often it is impossible for authorities to determine where these businesses are located. Many are located in Canada, Mexico, or offshore, which makes it difficult—if not impossible—for authorities to regulate. In 2006, the House Government Reform Committee held hearings on a bill requiring such Web sites to identify their locations as well as the names of doctors and pharmacists affiliated with the sites. The

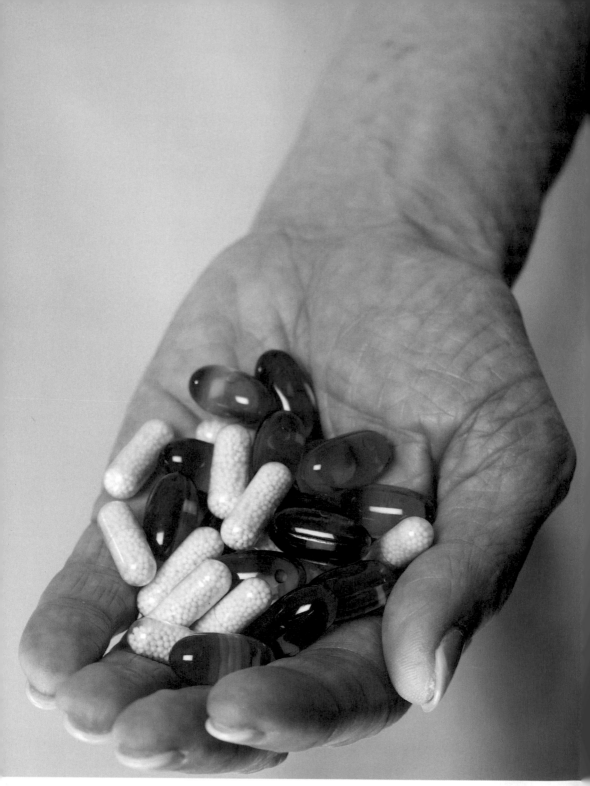

Monitor your own drug use whenever you're taking a prescribed medicine.

Rod Colvon, author of *Prescription Drug Addiction: The Hidden Epidemic*, recommends that patients take a more active role in their health care by following these steps:

- When prescribed any drug, ask your doctor if it's addictive. "Many people get hooked on prescription drugs merely because the don't realize the drug they're on is habit-forming," explains Colvin. "By knowing this from the outset, patients can avoid becoming addicts through sheer ignorance."
- If your family has a history of drug addiction or alcoholism, tell your doctor; it may mean that you're not a good candidate for the more addictive drugs or that you should be monitored more closely.
- If at any point you feel your doctor is not taking the time to fully understand your problems or explain your treatment and its side effects, insist on seeing a physician who will—if possible, someone who specializes in pain management, anxiety disorders, or addiction.
- If the drug you're being prescribed is habit forming, ask your doctor, "How quickly could I develop a dependence?" If you're on these drugs for this amount of time or longer, discuss with your doctor how you should taper off the drug to prevent withdrawal symptoms.
- While you're taking these drugs, monitor yourself for signs of addiction. Colvin suggests keeping these questions in mind: Have you ever felt that the amount of the drug you're prescribed isn't working as well as it used to? Do you experience more than just symptom relief on the drug, such as a feeling of excitement, or a "high"? Do you feel that you can perform certain tasks or activities (like driving in traffic or socializing at parties) only with the medication? If you answer yes to any of these questions, this may be a sign that you should broach the subject of addiction with your doctor.
- While on these drugs, ask three friends or family members to keep an eye on you as well. Say to them, "I'm on a medication that's potentially addictive. Can you tell me if you notice my personality changing over time—say, if I'm acting too happy, or more remote or irritable than usual?" The less secrecy and shame you have about using these drugs, the more likely you are to get help if you need it, says Colvin. "Most people understand alcoholism," he says. "But when an addict's drug of choice comes from a doctor, there's a lot more confusion. People think, Maybe she's supposed to be taking these. The more people who know that prescription drugs can be a problem, the faster we can stop this epidemic of addiction.

If a pharmacist sells a customer a medication without a prescription, he is committing a crime.

bill would also ban any sales made without an in-person consultation with a doctor and a valid prescription.

The White House Office of National Drug Control Policy ordered federal agencies with anti-drug programs to develop new strategies to combat prescription drugs' abuse and illegal marketing. According to director John P. Walters, "We don't want to wait until we get what we had with the crack epidemic. Hopefully we're a little bit earlier in the process."

Under the new plan, the FDA and DEA would have primary responsibility for the focus on prescription drugs. The Office of National Drug Control Policy asked the FDA to improve labeling for the most-often abused prescription drugs. Closure of online businesses, including pharmacies, selling drugs without prescriptions would be the responsibility of the DEA.

There have been rumblings that DTC advertising should be outlawed, or at the least, be more restricted. But pharmaceutical companies are big business, with vast financial holdings and much political influence, so any change in DTC regulations is not likely to happen soon.

Perhaps more likely to go into effect is a crackdown on what kind of "incentives" drug companies can give to health-care professionals for their consideration in prescribing their particular medications. Years ago—what may seem like centuries ago—pharmaceutical representatives might leave a few notepads, pens, pencils, calendars, or mugs at the doctor's office as not-so-subtle reminders about their products. Now, trips, machines, and other high-ticket items are left in the wake of sales representatives.

What role should sedatives play in our culture?

As the government, law enforcement, and honest doctors and pharmacists work together, they hope they will be able to stem the tide of prescription drug abuse.

Ultimately, some say, the argument goes back to Western culture's perception of medication and the role it plays—or should play—in people's lives. Have individuals become "soft," unable to handle stress or anxiety, letting it lead to sleepless nights? Is it too easy to pop a pill than to deal directly with problems—or to find other, nondrug solutions? Are sedative-hypnotics the solution—or the problem?

There can be no doubt that sedative-hypnotics play a major role in Western culture, and perhaps they play too big of a role. But they serve a valid purpose. The trick for the medical profession, law enforcement, and the consumer is to keep the role in balance.

U.S. Department of Justice Drug Enforcement Administration

Schedule I

- The drug or other substance has a high potential for abuse.
- The drug or other substance has no currently accepted medical use in treatment in the United States.
- There is a lack of accepted safety for use of the drug or other substance under medical supervision.
- Some Schedule I substances are heroin, LSD, and marijuana.

Schedule II

- The drug or other substance has a high potential for abuse.
- The drug or other substance has a currently accepted medical use in treatment in the United States or a currently accepted medical use with severe restrictions.
- Abuse of the drug or other substance may lead to severe psychological or physical dependence.
- Schedule II substances include morphine, PCP, cocaine, methadone, and methamphetamine.

Schedule III

- The drug or other substance has a potential for abuse less than the drugs or other substances in Schedules I and II.
- The drug or other substance has a currently accepted medical use in treatment in the United States.
- Abuse of the drug or other substance may lead to moderate or low physical dependence or high psychological dependence.

- Anabolic steroids, codeine and hydrocodone with aspirin or Tylenol, and some barbiturates are Schedule III substances.

Schedule IV

- The drug or other substance has a low potential for abuse relative to the drugs or other substances in Schedule III.
- The drug or other substance has a currently accepted medical use in treatment in the United States.
- Abuse of the drug or other substance may lead to limited physical dependence or psychological dependence relative to the drugs or other substances in Schedule III.
- Included in Schedule IV are Darvon, Talwin, Equanil, Valium, and Xanax.

Schedule V

- The drug or other substance has a low potential for abuse relative to the drugs or other substances in Schedule IV.
- The drug or other substance has a currently accepted medical use in treatment in the United States.
- Abuse of the drug or other substance may lead to limited physical dependence or psychological dependence relative to the drugs or other substances in Schedule IV.
- Over-the-counter cough medicines with codeine are classified in Schedule V.

(*Source*: From www.dea.gov.)

Glossary

abstinence: Restraint in indulging in a desire for something.

agoraphobia: A condition characterized by an irrational fear of public or open spaces.

anterograde: Affecting memories immediately following a shock, seizure, or ingesting of certain drugs.

anticonvulsant: Preventing or reducing seizures.

antihistamine: A drug that blocks cell receptors for histamine, either to prevent allergic reactions or to reduce the rate of certain secretions in the stomach.

anxiety: A state of intense apprehension or fear of real or imagined danger.

ataxia: The inability to coordinate the movements of muscles.

calmative: A drug or treatment that has a calming or quieting effect.

cardiologist: A doctor who specializes in the diagnosis and treatment of heart disorders and related conditions.

cardiorespiratory arrest: Stoppage of the heart and respiratory system.

chiral: Used to describe a molecule whose arrangement of atoms is such that it can't be superimposed on its mirror image.

chronic: Long-term or recurring frequently.

compulsive: Driven by an irresistible inner force to do something,

concomitant: Happening or existing along with or at the same time as something else.

consensus: General or widespread agreement among all members of a group.

controlled substances: Substances subject to legal control, especially a drug that can be obtained legally only with a prescription.

detoxification: The process of ridding the body of toxic substances.

efficacy: The ability to produce the desired effects.

endocrinologist: A doctor who treats disorders of the endocrine system.

epilepsy: A medical disorder characterized by episodes of abnormal electrical discharge in the brain and periodic sudden loss or impairment of consciousness, often with convulsions.

erratic: Unpredictable.

estrogen: Any of several steroid hormones, produced mainly in the ovaries, that stimulate estrus and the development of female secondary sexual characteristics.

exacerbated: Made an already bad situation worse.

hypertension: High blood pressure.

internist: A doctor who specializes in the diagnosis, prevention, and nonsurgical treatment of diseases affecting the internal organs.

intervention: An action taken to change what is happening or what might happen in someone else's life.

metabolites: Substances that are involved in or are by-products of metabolism.

neuroses: Mild psychiatric disorders characterized by anxiety, depression, and sometimes hypochondria.

panacea: A supposed cure-all for illnesses or other problems.

pharmacological: The science or study of drugs, including their sources, chemistry, production, use in treating diseases, and side effects.

protocol: The detailed plan of a scientific experiment, medical trial, or treatment.

REM *sleep:* The sleep stage that recurs several times during the night and is marked by dreaming, rapid eye movements (REM) under closed lids, and elevated pulse rate and brain activity.

seizure: The physical manifestation (such as convulsions, sensory disturbances, or loss of consciousness), resulting from an abnormal electrical discharge in the brain (as in epilepsy).

soluble: Able to be dissolved in liquid, especially water.

stupor: A state of greatly dulled senses.

synthesized: Combined different substances to create a new compound.

taper dosing: To gradually reduce the amount of a drug someone is taking with the purpose of eventually eliminating it completely.

vertigo: A condition in which someone feels a sensation of whirling or tilting that causes a loss of balance.

Further Reading

Clayton, Lawrence. *Barbiturates and Other Depressants*. New York: Rosen, 2001.

Derkins, Susie. *Barbiturates and Your Central Nervous System: The Incredibly Disgusting Story*. New York: Rosen, 2001.

Frisch, Carlienne. *When a Friend Has a Drug Problem*. New York: Rosen, 2000.

Gerdes, Louise I. *Addiction*. Farmington Hills, Mich.: Thomson Gale, 2004.

Houle, Michelle. *Tranquilizer, Barbiturate, and Downer Drug Dangers*. Berkeley Heights, N.J.: Enslow, 2001.

Hyde, Margaret O., and John F. Setaro. *Drugs 101*. Minneapolis, Minn.: Lerner, 2003.

Konieczko, Craig. *Intervention: Putting Yourself Between a Friend and Addiction*. New York: Rosen, 2000.

For More Information

Al-anon/Alateen
www.al-anon.org

Narcotics Anonymous
www.na.org

Parenting Teens
www.parentingteens.com/prescription_drug_abuse.html

Teens Health
kidshealth.org/teen/drug_alcohol/drugs/prescription_drug_abuse.
html

The websites listed on this page were active at the time of publication. The publisher is not responsible for websites that have changed their addresses or discontinued operation since the date of publication. The publisher will review and update the website list upon each reprint.

Bibliography

Drug Test Success. "Barbiturates." http://www.drugtestsuccess.com/barbiturates.htm.

eGetgoing. "Drug and Alcohol Information: Sedatives." http://www.egetgoing.com/drug_rehab/sedatives.asp.

Ekleberry, Sharon C. "Drug Module: Sedative-Hypnotics." http://www.toad.net/~arcturus/dd/sedative.htm.

HIPUSA—Mental Health. "Sedatives, Hypnotics, and Anxiolytics." http://www.hipusa.com/mentalhealth/sedatives.html.

"History of Barbiturates." http://www.chemcases.com/pheno/pheno01.htm.

"Medical Necessity Criteria for Substance Abuse and Dependence." *Clinical Care Guide.* Philadelphia: City of Philadelphia, 2000.

Missouri Department of Mental Health, Division of Alcohol and Drug Abuse. "As a Matter of Fact . . . Sedative Hypnotics." http://www.well.com/user/woa/fsseda.htm.

Psychology Today's Diagnosis Dictionary. "Sedative-Hypnotics." http://www.psychologytoday.com/conditions/index.php?term=sedative.

"Sedative-Hypnotics." http://www.addictionend.com/bookonline/4.htm.

Substance Abuse and Mental Health Services Administration. Overview of Findings from the 2004 National Survey on Drug Use and Health (Office of Applied Studies, NSDUH Series H-27, DHHS Publication No. SMA 05-4061). Rockville, Md.: U.S. Department of Health and Human Services, 2005.

Suzuki, Joji, Christopher L. Sola, and Olakunie Akinsoto. "Sedative, Hypnotic, Anxiolytic Use Disorders." http://www.emedicine.com/med/topic3119.htm.

Taylor, Guy. "OxyContin Abuse Becomes Scourge for Teens in Rural Areas." *Washington Times*, September 2, 2003.

Index

Picture Credits

Author and Consultant Biographies

Author

Ida Walker is a graduate of the University of Northern Iowa in Cedar Falls, and has done graduate work at Syracuse University in Syracuse, New York. The author of many nonfiction books, she lives in Upstate New York.

Series Consultant

Jack E. Henningfield, Ph.D., is a professor at the Johns Hopkins University School of Medicine, and he is also Vice President for Research and Health Policy at Pinney Associates, a consulting firm in Bethesda, Maryland, that specializes in science policy and regulatory issues concerning public health, medications development, and behavior-focused disease management. Dr. Henningfield has contributed information relating to addiction to numerous reports of the U.S. Surgeon General, the National Academy of Sciences, and the World Health Organization.